International Banking Strategic Alliances

International Banking Strategic Alliances

Reflections on BNP/Dresdner

Jörg Itschert

and

Rehan ul-Haq

First published 2003 by
PALGRAVE MACMILLAN
Houndmills, Basingstoke, Hampshire RG21 6XS and
175 Fifth Avenue, New York, N.Y. 10010
Companies and representatives throughout the world

PALGRAVE MACMILLAN is the global academic imprint of the Palgrave
Macmillan division of St. Martin's Press, LLC and of Palgrave Macmillan Ltd.
Macmillan® is a registered trademark in the United States, the United Kingdom
and other countries. Palgrave is a registered trademark in the European
Union and other countries.

ISBN 0–333–99259–8

This book is printed on paper suitable for recycling and made from fully
managed and sustained forest sources.

A catalogue record for this book is available from the British Library.

Library of Congress Cataloging-in-Publication Data
Itschert, Jörg.
    International banking strategic alliances / Jörg Itschert and Rehan ul-Haq.
        p.   cm.
    Includes bibliographical references and index.
    ISBN 0–333–99259–8
    1. Banks and banking, International.   2. International finance.
    I. ul-Haq, Rehan   II. Title.
    HG3881.I87 2003
    332.1′5—dc21   2003045687

10   9   8   7   6   5   4   3   2   1
12   11   10   09   08   07   06   05   04   03

Printed and bound in Great Britain by
Antony Rowe Ltd, Chippenham and Eastbourne

To patient Emeli, my greatest support

Jörg Itschert

To Aaminah and Lubna Sharmeen
Making my life worthwhile

Rehan ul-Haq

To the team at Palgrave Macmillan

The medal depicting the banking cooperation of Dresdner Bank and Banque Nationale de Paris

Source: Dresdner Bank Historical Archive, reproduced with permission.

Contents

Foreword

I have the honour of writing the Foreword for *International Banking Strategic Alliances*. The book is unique in a number of dimensions: it is a collaboration between Jörg Itschert (a German lawyer and banking practitioner) and Rehan ul-Haq (a British strategy academic); it is an insight, from the inside, into one of the major inter-country strategic alliances (between the French Banque Nationale de Paris – BNP – and the German Dresdner Bank); and it is a consideration of the major trends in banking, a core industry in the European project.

A number of factors undermine the ability of firms to achieve a sustainable long-run competitive advantage. These include deregulation and global competition. The norm has become short-run competitive advantage with frequent changes in the context leading to the need to continuously access new resources and capabilities. As new potential income streams open up, the banker makes decisions on how to capture these streams (by serving the needs of customers). The choices of 'how' range from acquisition to organic growth. The intermediate choice, the strategic alliance, is becoming more and more prevalent in all industries because of the speed of enactment and re-configuration.

At the core of the economic dimensions of the European project is the development of an open market: the free movement of goods, labour and capital. The increasing deregulation of the European banking industry (paralleled by increased regulation in protection for personal consumers) has made it possible to develop cross-border provision to follow trade and labour movements within Europe. The European Union (EU) and its member governments have facilitated increased competition in financial services through increasing the number of providers, and by increasing innovation through cross-border flows of knowledge and practice leading to reduced prices and improved products and services. Simultaneously the growth in strategic alliances has been monitored to ensure anti-trust situations do not arise.

BNP and Dresdner Bank had a prior history of collaboration in the clubs and consortium banks of the 1970s. When these organizations dissolved, BNP and Dresdner retained close relationships at board level and a lack of competition in their geographical structures. As new opportunities beckoned, the banks chose the 1988 joint World Bank/International Monetary Fund meeting in West Berlin to announce their collaboration.

Chapters 1 to 10 inclusive (Part I) document and examine the life-cycle of this alliance. The analysis provides insights into the regulatory hurdles at national and European levels, the development of a 'shared myth', the obstacles, the augurs as brand leaders, the possible end-point of the alliance turning into a merger, joint servicing of customers, Eastern European joint ventures, intercultural work and the dissolution of the alliance.

Chapters 11 to 14 inclusive (Part II) reflect on the insights that the BNP–Dresdner alliance provide into banking. Issues addressed include the cogency of the 'universal bank' model, the mechanisms for commercial banks to operate in overseas markets, the conflict between domestic and foreign cultures and markets and the outlook for international banking strategic alliances in the post-universal banking world.

Banking is reputed to be the industry with the greatest allocation of global capital. It is integral to the work of governments, international organizations (the UN, World Bank, Oxfam, the EU), multinationals, small and medium sized enterprises, households and individuals. Increasingly, trade links our world together and bankers underpin this through cross-border activities. The health of the banking system is therefore integral to our ability to achieve our goals.

This book is a welcome addition to our knowledge capital in this field. *International Banking Strategic Alliances* is written in an accessible manner and provides many insights into the practice and problems of collaboration. It uniquely documents the key issues in an alliance, seen from start to finish by an insider, and develops more general insights from the specific. This is a 'must read' for practitioners, policy-makers, academics and their students.

KAREL VAN MIERT
President Universiteit Nyenrode
Former EU Commissioner for Competition

Preface

During a meeting with the press in November 2001 (reported in *Handelsblatt*, No. 226, 22 November), the Chairman of Citigroup, Sir Winfried Bischoff, complained of a dearth of suitable takeover candidates on the European continent for his world-leading financial group. The banks, he explained, all suffer from the same disadvantage, namely that they are not 'pan-European institutions'. In fact, he added, they are present in only one or two markets at most, so that even Deutsche Bank is of no interest to Citigroup. The question nagging at him was probably why it should still be necessary to buy foreign banks one at a time: it would be far more convenient if one could buy a substantial presence on several national markets as a package deal (by the dozen, as it were).

What should a consultant say to that? Should he tell the would-be buyer he is right, and encourage him to stick by his search image? Or should the consultant put it to him that with such an approach he will probably have to keep on searching for a long time to come until the free play of market forces makes such an acquisition possible?

This gives rise to the question as to what 'element' might be capable of holding the desired dozen national banking presences together. The mere verbal creation of an artificial pan-European label will in itself not create its equivalent in reality. So where is the 'binding agent' for such supranational banking alliances supposed to come from? Assuming an imaginary multinational bank client had the power to achieve such a feat, his perfect anonymity would probably make it impossible to find him.

During an experiment that lasted ten years, BNP and Dresdner Bank set themselves the task of developing a suitable 'binding agent' which could be used as a permanent foundation for a transnational form of cooperation, but they failed to find a pan-European crystallization nucleus for such a banking alliance which could serve as a global 'fulcrum' in their operational business.

Part I will trace the individual phases this experiment ran through, focusing on the complex task as a whole. Detailed appraisals of specific processes or personal contributions could not be made the subject of research. It was relatively late before either party was confronted with the question of success or failure. At this moment of immeasurable disappointment, moreover, could one have expected them to make an authentic contribution to research into the reasons why the joint endeavour failed? Hardly, since they were unable to consider the issue 'from a distance'.

Now that a number of years have elapsed, the question again arises as to whether one can shed light on this complex of issues. The prospects of ascertaining what the causes really were are probably even less promising today than they were then, as now the protagonists no longer identify with the objectives of that time. The analyst seeking to determine why suitable ways and means of achieving the goal of a comprehensive, cross-border 'tandem solution' could not be found is left – speaking from the purely methodical viewpoint – only with the critical distance to the subject matter, although scientific investigations may provide the occasional hint. These questions will be dealt with in Part II.

There is no telling whether the agreement between BNP and Dresdner has lost its significance once and for all, but it is strange to note that there was no formal farewell between BNP's and Dresdner's international bankers. Certain organizational procedures were terminated and the joint property was divided up among the partners in such a way that each bank got back what it had previously developed and brought into the alliance. That was it. It had long been clear to both parties that banking had undergone paradigm shifts worldwide, the implications of which as yet remained to be seen before new clichés could be coined.

How did this book come to be written? By pure coincidence, Rehan ul-Haq paid Jörg Itschert a visit in his office just as the latter – having retired from banking in the meantime – was clearing his office of his personal belongings. Pointing to the stack of ring-binders on a trolley, Rehan asked, 'Since there won't be a successor for you, is all this going to end up as neatly filed fodder for the shredder?' A shrug of the shoulders by way of reply from Jörg. 'But this knowledge will remain fresh in your memory for a while to come, surely?' Answer: 'That's quite possible.' 'Then what's to stop you compiling an account of your experiences for interested scholars and practitioners? After all, it was people of learning who gave you the wherewithal to get this job in the first place and your colleagues helped to develop your knowledge. Wouldn't it be fair to give back the experience you have gathered in return? How else can one be sure that investments in this sector are put to the proper use?' Hesitant answer: 'I suppose I could give it a try.' 'Fantastic! If you like, I could help you with it.' 'You're on!'

JÖRG ITSCHERT
REHAN UL-HAQ

List of Abbreviations

ABECOR	Associated Banks of Europe Corporation
ABN	Algemene Bank Nederland
AGM	Annual General Meeting
BAKred	German Federal Banking Authority
BIS	Bank for International Settlements
BKA	German Cartel Authority
BNL	Banca Nazionale de Lavoro
BNP	Banque Nationale de Paris
BoA	Bank of America
CEE	central and eastern Europe
CEO	Chief Executive Officer
CNEP	Comptoir Nationale d'Escompte de Paris
HR	human resources
ICC	International Chamber of Commerce
IT	information technology
JV	joint venture
PDG	Président-Directeur Générale
PR	public relations
SBF	strategic business field
SBU	strategic business unit
SFE	Société Financière Européenne

Part I

Flawed International Banking Alliance: Case Study on BNP/Dresdner Bank Cooperation

1
Multilateral Banking Cooperation as a Means of Participating in Multinational Link-ups

Specifying the topic

Since, in a global, monetary context, any occurrence tends to have its cause in the banking world, it would be useful to begin by defining a precise thematic framework.

The following aspects will be disregarded:

- explicit forms of ad hoc cooperation in international operations
- foreign networks of one and the same banking group
- investment banking, managed from international financial centres, which by nature tends towards a supranational networking.

Turning to the topic at hand, the fundamental question that presents itself is this: if a bank were to enter into a cooperation agreement with a complementary foreign partner, would it be possible to access a broader spectrum of foreign customers through an organization created jointly with that partner under a strategic alliance forged for an unlimited period of time? And could a bank, in squaring up to such a challenge, gradually cease giving (the totally natural) priority to its own domestic activities to assume the characteristics of a – primarily – internationally operating institution? The latter would, of course, take place to the extent to which transnational market structures in Europe and throughout the world gradually gained the upper hand.

Over the last 20 years, a great many banks with supraregional and international business operations no doubt considered questions of this kind, yet without coming to conclusions along the lines of a cross-border strategic alliance. The main reason for this is almost certainly that they did not try to find a partner at random. In a rapidly changing world of finance, experience tells us this is virtually inconceivable.

That the link between BNP (Banque Nationale de Paris) and Dresdner Bank was an exception to the rule and the reason that these banks could quite happily make their unparalleled project public in 1990 was due to the fact that during the 1980s they had built up a partnership by degrees and in a number of phases, enabling them to get to know each other. When the two institutions eventually decided to present themselves to the world as allies, all it took was one final step in a development that had begun a decade before.

Institutionalized cooperation between foreign banks before 1990

The history of international banking following the Second World War is closely linked to monetary developments and the growing deregulation towards freely convertible currencies. The banks saw their main task as being to help their customers – for the most part companies from their own country – to stimulate foreign trade.

Compared to the time between the world wars, a general breakthrough in the direction of efficient foreign exchange trading was achieved at the beginning of the 1950s. This allowed the banks to spend less time acting as watchdogs by appointment of their central bank. Instead, once their domestic business networks had been rebuilt, they were able to turn their attention to building up lasting ties abroad.

If one considers the political reservations that were harboured towards foreign capital, it becomes clear why the nationalization of the banks was a common economic policy measure as a means of ensuring that the rebuilding of the economy proceeded safely and with all due correctness. As the banks at this time, whether state-owned or private, spent most of their time issuing foreign-trade documentation, they initially restricted their contacts abroad to cultivating relations with a select circle of correspondent banks from which they hoped, moreover, for assistance with transfers and in making investments. Once, by the 1950s, a transnational money market had developed around the clearing system of foreign banks in the form of fungible US dollar deposits with US banks and other convertible currencies, more openings were created for the commercial banks of the western world to engage in funding abroad.[1]

Multilateral forms of cooperation in commercial banking of the 1970s

The laborious practice of bilateralism led to the general realization that true progress in international banking was only to be achieved with multinational concepts (often termed clubs and consortium banks) following the example of the political development of the European Communities. In the second half of the 1960s, many sought the answer in the magic formula 'banking cooperation'. The astonishing progress of the European Economic Community (EEC) at that time, with its six member states, gave the biggest three or four banks in each member state the idea of forming multilateral ties with each other. The outcome was the arrival, virtually overnight, of several competing clubs of banks (SFE, EUROPARTNERS, EBIC, ORION, INTERALPHA), whereby each national banking industry was represented in each club through one well-known bank.

Each club proceeded to set up a joint 'financing vehicle' with bank status and a base in an international banking centre (London or Paris). These were generally referred to as 'syndicate banks'. Their main activity comprised revolving syndicated loans on the basis of Euro-deposits with the help of which – from the mid-1970s – petrodollars were channelled back into the international banking circulation. Later on, syndicate banks with mixed shareholder groups consisting of European and Middle East institutions predominated, which was a formation considered particularly well suited to dispelling the tensions that the oil price shocks of 1975 and 1981 had brought to the international financial markets.

BNP, which resulted in 1967 from the merger of two venerable national institutions and advanced to become market leader in the French domestic market, and Dresdner Bank, Germany's second-largest bank, first came into contact with one another as members of the select international club of banks with the name 'Société Financière Européenne' (SFE). The other members were Barclays Bank, Banca Nazionale de Lavoro (BNL), Algemene Bank Nederland (ABN) and the Banque de Bruxelles, with the Bank of America (BoA) as a transatlantic partner. A joint subsidiary company with banking status was founded in Paris under the style 'Banque SFE', and was assisted by an SFE holding company with its seat in Luxembourg.

From the mid-1970s – BoA had just pulled out – the private joint stock banks ABN, Banque de Bruxelles, Barclays and Dresdner (together with Bayerische Hypo) embarked on a new, promising road without resigning from the SFE. They believed that the reason for the lamentable immobility of the SFE lay in the lack of autonomy of the 'state-owned banks'. Hence the attempt to achieve through a further club, which was given the name 'ABECOR' (Associated Banks of Europe Corporation) – initially without the state-owned banks BNP and BNL – everything SFE had prevented them from achieving. Unlike SFE, ABECOR was not to compete with its members in connection with projects for which tenders were invited internationally. Instead, ABECOR would act as a vehicle for communicating the intra-group expertise it possessed to its members for training purposes, thereby strengthening the members' clout in the international banking arena. A joint secretariat was set up in Brussels, the European capital, with the task of bringing together specialists from the various banking arms to meet in working groups. Not only did these meetings give colleagues from different countries an opportunity to exchange experience, but they promoted a sense of shared identity as well.

In the mid-1970s, the Arabian/European syndicate bank BAII was founded in Paris under the auspices of BNP and Dresdner Bank. The shareholdings were split more or less equally between Europe and the Middle East. Moreover, a Latin American/European syndicate bank was established in London. Its name was Eulabank, and BNP and Dresdner were involved in it, too.

Poor marks for the European banking clubs

The banking clubs had a thankless task to perform. Although they did develop, the immense expectations their members placed on them due to imprecise notions of what international banking was all about could not be fulfilled. For the members, the important thing was to be seen on their home markets as having a 'truly international' flair, a condition that was not necessarily satisfied due to the equal status given to all members of the club. Further, the business rewards of such a membership were paltry given that the small participations in the respective group vehicles turned out to be – apart from the credit risks – irrelevant in terms of earnings. What is more, the individual members were not able to translate to the desired extent the special strength they had, namely their predominant position on their home markets, into influence with the management of the syndicate bank.

On the acquisitions side, the brokering of large loans (syndicated loans) on the international syndicated sector was completely different from the domestic markets in any case. Repeat borrowers took advantage of the number of banks available by carefully spreading their demand, and selectively exploited local practices, giving outsiders little chance of involvement. Thus, club membership produced hardly any business benefits.

Basically, the bottom line of the joint strategy of the European banking clubs was to derive as much prestige and strategic gain as possible from the privilege of exclusiveness and to boost members' egos by making each feel elevated to a higher international plain. Their common objective was also to publicly seize upon tantalizing topics in the hope that this would enhance their appeal to prospective customers. The actual value of personal ties at international level was scarcely to be compared, however, with the influence wielded in local markets.

Another hope was, of course, to bring personal influence to bear when it came to putting attractive syndications together; yet there was essentially little justification for such hopes for, when it came to Eurobond issues, the ability to place bonds successfully under difficult market conditions became the prime prerequisite and was rewarded with the appropriate positions.

Fruits of Associated Banks of Europe Corporation disappoint

Compared with the respectable position the member banks commanded on their local markets, the fruits of participation in the ABECOR Working Groups had a sobering effect. With the exception of the economists, who regularly and intensively exchanged thoughts on all the foreign markets and were able to tap into sizeable databases and analysis capacities on a reciprocal basis, expectations were generally not met. The pluralism of opinions was one particular irritant that became obvious in a group of five to seven banks when projects had to be evaluated and realized. In most cases, a larger number of banks in agreement were held back by stubborn minorities. This suggested that efficient structures were possible only with a much smaller number of members.

One enduring accomplishment of the ABECOR cooperation turned out to be ABIN, the joint training centre in Bad Homburg, Germany, where specialist seminars involving the members' junior executives were offered with English and French as the working languages. Participation, moreover, contributed to a certain community spirit.

De facto 'twinning' of Banque Nationale de Paris and Dresdner Bank

When, at the end of the 1980s, the above syndicate banks had to be liquidated, it was BNP and Dresdner who did the bulk of the work. This would scarcely have been possible if the two banks had not collaborated closely. In addition, committee work in SFOM, a joint holding company in Geneva for a number of African subsidiary banks, and a joint venture in Turkey, BNP–AK-Dresdner Bank AS, Istanbul, gave them further opportunities to establish a common decision-making practice and closer contacts, not just personally but also at company level. During the course of regular board meetings, for example, a relationship of trust grew among board members with foreign banking responsibilities, their meetings forming the backdrop for a regular exchange of opinions on, and experience in, foreign matters.

Experience in the geographical expansion of each other's activities within the EU led to similarities in how they came to view strategic questions over time. Whereas they originally saw, given the increasing interconnections in Franco–German trade, a reason for planning a wide-ranging local presence on either side of the Rhine, they formed a completely different opinion of the situation towards the end of the 1980s. Both banks considered the relationship of trust that resulted from a largely competitive neutrality in their third-country activities as a blessing, a particular stroke of luck. This may be best described by the French word *jumelage*, which had established itself at local level for years. In this experience they saw confirmation that profitable cooperation was indeed possible only via a partnership of two. For when, within the scope of an alliance, several partners had to be given their say, conflicting viewpoints were bound to impair the efficiency of such an organization.

The happy coincidence of this relationship of mutual trust, then, was felt to be a privilege other banks did not have and, as such, a development that left the others far behind. It is therefore not surprising that BNP and Dresdner occasionally gave some thought as to how this cutting edge in foreign business might be put to even better use in terms of promoting not just their image but their business activities as well. The first joint summit of the World Bank and the International Monetary Fund (IMF) in Europe, held in West Berlin in 1988, was the setting chosen to announce the intention to take their cooperation still further. In a series of interviews it was explained to the financial press that whatever BNP did on the cooperation front in future, it was absolutely clear that Dresdner was the only partner that came into consideration. Only a few months later the two banks surprised the public by announcing cross-administrative and supervisory board mandates. Given BNP's status as a state-owned bank, this was looked upon as nothing less than sensational.

Profiles of the partner banks on the eve of forming the alliance

Before the beginnings of the alliance are described, it seems appropriate to recap where the two banks found themselves, strategy-wise, at that point in time and to review in broad strokes how they got there.

The business interests of Dresdner Bank

It seems appropriate to start with Dresdner, which in this initial phase assumed the role of driving force. The reason for this lies probably in the fact that debate in the French banking sector at that time was still far too involved with issues of economic policy liberalism, the privatization of the nationalized banks and so on, to take the theoretical initiative in foreign banking.

The German bank, which was happy to oblige, should really have had enough on its plate with the dramatic turn of political events brought on by the fall of the Berlin Wall and reunification in 1989/90. One might have thought that the large German banks in particular – first and foremost Dresdner with its traditional links to Saxony and Prussia – would have been so focused on winning back their old territory that they had absolutely no 'grey cells' left to think of revolutionizing their foreign activities.

Oddly enough this was not the case, suggesting that this extra intellectual workload taken on by Dresdner in particular was intended as a way of placing the problems of its foreign operations – including the changes taking place outside its own door to the east – into the hands of the partnership with BNP for a period of five to ten years, allowing the bank to concentrate on the problems cast up by reunification. Faced with this conflict of interests between domestic and foreign business, Dresdner was in no doubt that the true challenge of the moment lay in the new federal states of east Germany, and that this challenge could not be put off or dealt with superficially. This was so obvious to the bank that it was anxious to counteract the impression that, because of the pressing tasks facing it at home, it had already placed the development of its operations abroad on the back burner for an indefinite period of time.

In retrospect, Dresdner Bank was unable to disguise the fact that, compared with the days before the First World War, since the market crash at the end of the 1920s it was no longer truly at home in foreign banking. Under the patriarchal regime of Karl Goetz, the bank's rescuer in 1929 and initiator of the rebuilding in the west after 1945, foreign business was seen at all times as a necessary evil, which is to say that investments were made only out of consideration for the foreign trade engaged in by its important large customers.

The most appropriate tactic, then, was surely to announce to an astonished public a message along the lines of: 'We are planning to give an entirely new and modern slant to our foreign business operations in future, and under our new "banner", the partnership with BNP, our equal-ranking ally which has considerable experience in foreign banking, we are willing to take the inevitable steps required by the dual challenge, these being European monetary union envisaged under the Maastricht Treaty and the globalization of the financial and capital markets.' Seen from this perspective, forming a strategic alliance with a European partner of equal rank represented the fast route to the twenty-first century.

Company history and interests of BNP

Following on from what has been said above concerning the development of the nationalized banks in France, it was possible to differentiate between two 'classes' of nationalized banks. The first, the 'nobler class', dated back to 1947, and the second to 1982. The founder banks of BNP, CNEP (Comptoir Nationale d'Escompte de Paris) and BNCI (Banque Nationale pour le Commerce et l'Industrie) belonged to the first category. BNP came about as a result of the merger of these two institutions in 1966. One factor favouring this merger was the complementary structure of the two founder institutions. On the other hand, the timing of the merger proved to be perfect, as it gave the French banking sector unparalleled new stimulus.

As a powerful arm of the French Ministry of Finance, the BNP took advantage of every opportunity to expand the impressive network of foreign branches it had inherited to take care of the foreign side of financing France's international trade. After the conservative government began privatizing state-owned banks with Société Générale in 1988, BNP's ambition to make greater profits on the international markets as a large privatized bank grew. Moreover, the bank was experiencing the same profitability problems with domestic operations as affected virtually all of Europe's big credit institutions, prompting the management of BNP to emphasize its outstanding foreign network as a particular asset.

This network of important foreign bases – often with a century-old tradition under one of the two founder banks – had been the fulcrum of France's foreign trade activities, especially in times of exchange-rate policy tensions. The soundness of these foreign branches also encouraged BNP to woo customers in third countries whenever the local credit industry showed scope for development (for example, in leasing). Seen in this light, a global agreement with Dresdner Bank to cater to the needs also of Dresdner's customers at locations where Dresdner did not maintain a presence had its positive aspects.

The beginnings of the joint strategy concept

At the end of 1989 a meeting was held in Paris involving all the members of Dresdner's Board of Managing Directors and BNP's Comité de Direction. Their joint analysis of the developments on the banking and finance markets worldwide revealed a high degree of consensus which would be deepened the following year by holding brain-storming sessions on individual topics. In mid-1990 Dresdner set down the thoughts thus arrived at in a cross-divisional position paper. Containing, in key words, the fundamental principles of a strategic alliance, an English translation of this paper was handed over to BNP for comment.

BNP had no basic objections to this position paper. The joint objective and the means of achieving it were convincingly sketched, and neither was there any categorical resistance from the division heads of the two banks, to whom the confidential paper was passed. For this reason, the paper was later given the pleasant-sounding name 'Magna Carta'. As early as the final quarter of 1990, an editing committee at Dresdner set about drafting first proposals for contractual provisions. Beforehand, the individual divisions had been called upon to give their opinion on what they felt needed to be regulated via a contractual agreement.

In retrospect, this (to all intents and purposes) problem-free process of reaching an agreement begs the question whether the two partners allowed themselves to be swept along on a wave of euphoria without having reached, in theory and empirically, an adequate understanding of the functional interrelationships. For example, neither partner suggested pilot projects to look for particularly well-suited means of creating a union. The problems involved should, first of all, have been examined and analysed more closely to obtain a feel for the true dimensions of this vast undertaking.

What is more, the German bank would have done well to look into how BNP's agreement was meant. Instead, it immediately proclaimed that the

French saw the situation and the task at hand as the Germans did, and in fact thought like the Germans. Yet BNP had intended merely to express a friendly 'Well done!' for getting the ball rolling. Absolutely no conclusions for the course of what might prove to be a gripping ongoing dialogue were to be drawn – heaven forbid! – from that. Certainly, it was too early to conclude, according to a strictly Cartesian understanding of reality, that the ideal solution was already in view. *Courtoisie* (Courtly Conduct) and *politesse* (Politeness) had demanded that the first signs of such a delicate shoot be given a warm round of applause.

The Germans, however, read BNP's response as complete agreement, at least in principle. It did not occur to anyone that this might be a case of 'hidden dissidence', meaning the banks may have thought they had agreed on certain ideas that could not be judged properly until much later. *Honi soi qui mal y pense* (Shame on negative intentions)! Apart from that, each partner was extremely anxious to let discretion prevail for fear of upsetting the other. Certainly, in this state of euphoria neither bank was in a position to realize that they were entering new ground, a *terra incognita* full of pitfalls that would one day develop into an ice-floe that had broken loose.

Note

1. When this resulted in the trading of securitized Eurobonds, an autonomous, globally tolerated Eurocapital market ensued, with market volumes that grew year after year and a homogeneous, global investment banking environment that offered worldwide investment opportunities in various currencies and maturity categories. In terms of organization, the globally uniform standards of this truly international market were undoubtedly a historic achievement. Yet the fact that settlement and custody were often executed off-shore to side-step national income taxes created more and more difficulties in times of low economic growth and increasingly stringent international agreements to combat money laundering.

2
A New Brand of International Banking Alliance

The principles behind the cooperation agreement

When two protagonists plan to cooperate in important areas of their business activities, such an intention could be expressed in a simple contractual agreement covering the measures that are without doubt to be taken in the foreseeable future, based on the realistic understanding that the means and objectives may be adjusted to the prevailing situation at any given time. To stipulate certain expectations beforehand, however, contradicts the strategic maxim of avoiding unnecessary provisos at all costs.

Other rules applied to the alliance of BNP and Dresdner Bank. Since legal experts had warned that the full wording of the cooperation agreement would, in a competitive European environment, at some point have to be made public, the two partners decided to take advantage of this fact to achieve an optimal public reaction. The purpose of the contractual negotiations, then, was not to outline projects that were ripe for implementation. Instead, the two banks painted a rather vague, expansive vision of the future, the aim being to demonstrate that they were capable of thinking 'across national borders' with all due consideration for global implications. Different scenarios were presented as to how – through a mysterious, joint headquarters in a third country – commercial banking units in all corners of the globe might interact to create a joint foreign group, the structure of which would reflect the interests of both partners equally and satisfy the needs of the corporate clients of both institutions.

This concept's true significance lay in the context of the process of European integration in the guise of the imminent European monetary union, of which the partner banks considered themselves to be the true exponents. Moreover, BNP and Dresdner wanted to give their backing to the globalization tendencies of the currency, financial and credit markets. All this seemed to be within reach in the historic haze that was 1990. Hence the need to act quickly, lest two other renowned banks of different national origin and of similar size beat them to it with a similar concept. Their place in history as banking pioneers was at stake.[1]

The importance of presenting the alliance under a joint 'banner'

Wherever joint operational units were established, the chief concern was to outwardly project a uniform corporate image. This development was to culminate in the creation of a joint holding company with the stature of a universal bank which, as the incarnation of this corporate image, was to forge ahead with the task of creating a more homogeneous joint branch network with maximum earning power.

Cooperation was to take place at three levels.

1 Determining the objectives of the cooperation was to be the responsibility of the top hierarchy level of each bank.
2 Joint ventures were to have an autonomous management level.
3 Horizontal product- and infrastructure-related projects had to be agreed on and steered by the responsible board member.

The subject matter of the agreement: the full product range of a universal bank

The alliance partners consciously refrained from selecting from the business sectors traditionally covered by universal banks which activities were suitable for joint operations in a third country and which were not. Time would tell which sectors were best suited to cooperation. In the meantime, the field of activity of the strategic alliance was deemed to be global and all-inclusive, although clearly defined activities could be excluded at any time if expressly agreed by both banks.

Each partner's domestic activities off-limits for the cooperation

The dividing line between foreign operations and domestic operations was not wholly free of misunderstandings. It seemed to make little sense that the very quality that gave the banks stature as big banks on their respective home markets should be studiously left out of the decision-making process within the scope of the partnership. On the other hand, it was clear that the inclusion of excessive competition on the two home markets (which took totally different forms in each country) in the lumbering consultation process was virtually impossible because something had to be done, and time was of the essence. Furthermore, a large number of individual transactions, particularly in commercial banking, concluded by both partners abroad were directly linked to domestic customers, making a separation of the two impossible. Drawing a clear dividing line between the two fields of operation proved to be far more difficult, in theory and in practice, than first assumed.

The involvement of product specialists in the executive of the alliance

One special feature of this new brand of cooperation was the active involvement of product specialists. This the banking partners intended as a rejection of earlier forms of cooperation that were based on a practice-remote dogma whereby the presidents and 'foreign ministers', far removed from the hurly-burly on their executive floors, decided what was good for the cooperation.

This approach was also born out of the conviction that a large number of parallel initiatives and processes were needed to get a joint venture off the ground. The partners hoped that the interplay of their sales networks, inspired by the know-how and commitment of middle management, would quickly come up with innovative products. For this reason it was decided that the latter be offered a legitimate place within the executive of the alliance, the 'Commission'. Yet it was impossible to formulate a clear-cut definition of just how far the product specialists' involvement in the decision-making process, which was desirable in principle, should go. The idea was that the line should be drawn pragmatically via their delegation to the Commission, as opposed to the 'Regular Meetings' of both management boards (supervisory body). Indeed, this arrangement meant that the bottom-up principle was embraced by the alliance, at least in theory.

Opposite numbers at the parent banks

At first, it was taken for granted that word would quickly spread at both organizations as to how the respective functional responsibilities were allocated at the other partner bank. After all, coordination as a bureaucratic process was supposed somehow to bring together the parties concerned. However, these expectations were not fulfilled due to numerous incongruencies between the nomenclatures within the two organizational structures and different correlations of individual groups or units within the respective organizational set-ups. In practice, this meant that in most cases, individuals delegated by their organization to participate in specific meetings could only explain at length that although such-and-such a thing had also cropped up at their bank, they themselves no longer had anything to do with it, and that it was the responsibility of someone else they did not know personally.

Main purpose of the alliance: bringing units in third countries together

There is no overlooking in the cooperation agreement (cf. Appendix 1) the special importance attached to the merging of operational units in third countries, a basic tenet that runs through the text like a red thread. Up to roughly 1995, it was mutually agreed that the real implementation of the strategic alliance should take place – with the exception of the joint ventures in central and eastern Europe (CEE) – within this context, step by step according to meticulously stated principles. The partners would start with the units in countries where both maintained a presence, then capital would be injected and staff made available to turn individually run presences into joint units. Parallel to these developments, the cooperating banks were to invest in new joint banks (joint ventures) in regions that were new territory for both parties (for example, in CEE).

Avoiding the overlap of responsibilities within the alliance

The main problem that had previously dogged multilateral banking alliances was that competencies at the partner banks and the joint venture units of the alliance overlapped. For a bilateral banking alliance that had set itself the task of establishing a joint, integrated third-country bank under a central management unit, there was in principle no such problem, unless the process of establishing and building up the controlling unit – the 'large holding' – ran into delays.

This was most certainly the case from 1996 onwards, which radically changed the concept of the alliance. The principle of a joint market approach remained intact, as did the principle of joining forces in countries in which neither partner had an operational unit. But all the other constellations failed to eliminate an overlap of responsibilities between divisions and departments of the respective partner banks or between one of the partners and a joint unit, depending on the business division and customer segment. These would inevitably lead to energy-sapping clashes within the alliance. Since the alliance intended to remain open, it was possible for a prolonged period of time to dodge the issue of when and how the paralysing effect of overlaps might be remedied once and for all by partially merging group subsidiaries.

Status of the staff involved in the alliance

The final stage envisaged by the cooperation agreement was the establish-ment of a legally independent subsidiary bank, owned by two equal-ranking shareholders, as a holding company. This subsidiary was to be governed by an elite, a multinational group of executives who were to be given control over their staff as well as extensive business policy autonomy. To redress the balance, the members of the Commission of the alliance would sit on the supervisory boards of these subsidiary banks to ensure that business policy at the subsidiaries was in line with that applicable to the alliance as a whole. The provisions governing the powers with which the holding company was to be endowed were to have been set down in a separate agreement between the partner banks. No final draft of such an agreement ever materialized, as the partners were unable to reach a consensus on where the future holding company should be based.

Until the holding company was up and running, the executive staff were to be appointed on a case-by-base basis by equal-ranking executive teams from both partner banks. Staffing suggestions from the other side were carefully considered, although priority was given to candidates with experience relevant to the alliance. A candidate's ability to establish a relationship of trust with customers from the other bank was the most important prerequisite. Joint new appointments for certain purposes of the alliance were sometimes made under temporary contracts. All other employment relationships were governed by local labour laws.

The makeshift solution of temporarily delegating expatriates did not always suit the purpose of the alliance. After a number of years spent abroad, the personal interests of such staff were focused on returning to their home bank to further their career rather than on the advancement of the alliance.

Ongoing conflict between dogmatic self-promotion and strategic shrewdness

It goes without saying that radical concepts, such as the formation of a strategic alliance between two globally operating banking groups with more than 50,000 employees, call for individuals with strong communication skills. The purpose of such a task is patently obvious, as only people who are convincing and convinced are able to sell such a complex concept to a mutual customer. Yet this is a task involving certain pitfalls, since one can easily overshoot the mark in the indoctrination process in as much as dogmas may come into being that run counter to the fundamental strategic intention of keeping the necessary manoeuvrability in competition open as an option.

Often it is the people addressed who look for further reasons to make a certain thing appear more plausible and impressive. For example, if the question asked is: 'Why are we predestined to do such-and-such and not some-one else?', they will come up with convincing reasons why they are special. The resulting self-stylizations in the form of ideological fixations can bear strange fruit in the consciousness of the general public, for once the public has formed a certain explanation for the specific approach of the alliance they are loath to give it up, and may even embellish upon certain aspects. But when developments in competition take an unexpected turn, it is extremely difficult to adjust the strategy, as there is then the risk that the public may be disappointed by the actual reaction, having imagined the preconditions for success too much in terms of the old style. The public does not usually look kindly on such stylistic lapses.

On the other hand, the dogmatized formulae are often overemphasized truisms or perfectionist exaggerations, the accentuation of which seems most primitive. If one examines the agreement more closely from this viewpoint, one will detect many cases of fixations of principles which, as a result of dogmatized expectations, may lead to self-imposed blocks, for these are what greatly restricts flexibility of reaction.

The following examples of irrefutable dogmas may serve to illustrate this point.

1   The dogma of the superiority of an exclusive bilateral relationship (without opening clauses).
2   The dogma of the progressiveness of Franco–German joint ventures.
3   The dogma of perfect parity ('as equal partners with absolute and sustained parity').
4   The dogma of the need to defuse conceivable conflict situations beforehand by way of evasive procedures.
5   The dogma of a uniform, globally applicable valuation standard for merged units and of the consideration payable in this respect.
6   The dogma of the automatic liquidation of joint units if profit targets are not met after more than two years.

The meaning and purpose of most of the above generalizations as dogmatisms are more or less self-explanatory, but it is more difficult to imagine what rules for avoiding conflicts might be. Chosen as a precaution, these are procedures under which both parties are to undertake the same type of efforts to neutralize or objectify the critical situation in question, the aim being to avoid a potential conflict in the sense of a conceivable clash of ethnocentric positions at the expense of the position of the alliance. The following examples may serve to illustrate this more clearly.

First of all, the establishment of a joint holding company was envisaged as the keystone both of an efficient joint organization and of a global management of the alliance's third-country operations. But where was it to be situated? Paris and Frankfurt were out of the question, as otherwise the notion of an alliance of equals would be cast in doubt. The dictates of a fair mutual consensus between the partners therefore ruled out having the seat in France or Germany. The solution could only be to set up the joint holding company in a conveniently located third country. Other criteria had to be considered. For example, the venue would have to be a recognized financial centre and have liberal tax laws. Since, as has already been said, the partners never did reach an agreement, it will never be known whether Brussels or Luxembourg – the latter being the Germans' first choice – would have won the day.

An even more delicate issue surrounded the language problem. Which partner, the French or the German banker, could in principle have been made to express himself in writing in the mother tongue of the other? And at German banks and companies, the principle of common law applies: *quot non est in actis, non est in mundo* (Whatever is not mentioned in the files, does not exist in the world). This led to the Solomonic decision to choose a third language, English, as the 'language of the cooperation', based on the assumption that since both sides had comparable educational backgrounds the recognized lingua franca would, as the language for bankers worldwide, cause them the same difficulties.

The agreement of a globally uniform valuation standard for the merging of operational units in third countries constituted a Utopian joint postulation. Apparently, each bank mistrusted the other's traditional business model yet, in cases of doubt, the company laws applicable locally were to provide the solution for questions of valuation. Since the responsible local auditors were also bound by the local laws, there was in reality no scope for deviating arrangements.

The person least likely to benefit from such dogmatism was the customer for, if an esteemed medium-sized corporate client lacking Anglo-Saxon business experience visits a joint venture (JV) branch in person, rather than engage in English conversation what he wants is an experienced fellow-countryman who can give him the advice he needs.

The ultimate consequence of such evasive action is usually that for fear of conceivable moot points, new – and in the long run, perhaps greater – obstacles are erected. In such a case it would be easier to call on the services of a neutral solicitor with experience in this line of business.

'No handle against the hidden enemies of the cooperation'

The tactic adopted by the self-protective, anti-cooperation strategists in both camps was as effective as it was simple: namely, to 'work to rule'. If the regulations were not satisfied meticulously and beyond all measure of doubt, the hands of the individual involved were found to be 'unfortunately' tied. Opportunities particularly well-suited for throwing a spanner in the works came in the form of exceptionally pliable principles such as absolute equality of status, or formalistic criteria such as coordination requirements between the two head offices. Moreover, by taking this stance it was even possible to behave with impunity as an apparent supporter of the alliance.

Why dispense with an integration-promoting, joint symbol of identity?

When manufacturers have their products sold in different countries they use a symbol (logo) to establish a link between their identity and their products. This being so, it comes as a surprise that two contracting parties from a services sector were unable, given their strategic alliance of unlimited duration, finally to agree on a logo under which they could present themselves to the market together. It is even more of a mystery that this should be so in such an overcrowded sector, where readily identifiable symbols are more important than in any other.

In the above instance, the two partners apparently chose not to look for a symbol agreeable to both because their respective local symbols could have suffered had a joint logo become firmly implanted in the customers' consciousness. This is probably why they lacked the courage to create an original (and competitive) third symbol. The previous era of banking cooperation clearly still had a disconcerting effect. Commerzbank, for example, continued to use the 'EUROPARTNERS' logo as its own after officially terminating its cooperation, because the shared logo was so firmly lodged in the customers' mind.

Note

1. Strangely enough, unlike industrialists, who think in terms of market shares and profit rates, there are bankers who are driven primarily by the desire to go down in history. When they can stick out their chests and say: 'And we were the first to embark on such a project!' they believe they can sit back and relax, satisfied that the most important part of their work has been done. Their foremost priority is to create the impression that every conceivable detail was taken into consideration with the utmost methodical care and both eyes fixed on the future.

3
Shareholders and the EC Commission give the Go-ahead

This chapter concerns 'folkloristic' pastimes of the young (West German) Federal Republic without it having anything to do with the assertion of the German bank's business interests. Three 'holy' key phrases sum up this special set of circumstances: shareholder democracy, regulatory politics and antitrust legislation. As a matter of fact, in German economic policy at that time there was scarcely anything more important for journalists to cast their Argus eye (careful and severe eye) upon. The times demanded that something exemplary be produced in all three respects. Great care was called for with all three virtues, as no good could be expected to come of them.

It has already been implied that the purpose of the cooperation agreement was largely to serve as a public relations (PR) weapon. It was particularly well-suited to this purpose in that it bore a clear resemblance to a manifesto directed at a number of targets outside the partnership: the shareholders, the capital markets, the EU Commission in its capacity of Fair Trade Authority as well as public opinion as such, by referring to such highly topical issues as European integration and the globalization of the domestic markets. All this material ultimately served to promote the image of the partners as if to say: 'Look at us, we're the first to do anything for the banking markets that are growing together in Europe and worldwide!'

With typical missionary zeal, the partners did not want to feed the public just with key words, but to present and implement a detailed blueprint that took pioneering steps in several directions. To be more precise, by providing sophisticated scenarios they sought not only to emphasize their competence in these matters but to claim, once and for all, in the consciousness of the public the copyright for the shaping of this futuristic material.

Including the shareholders in the cross-border alliance

As has already been said, it was considered a particular duty at Dresdner, as befits a true shareholder democracy, to inform the highest authority governing the German share, the annual general meeting (AGM) of shareholders, of the concept behind the alliance which (and of this Dresdner had not the slightest doubt) was of outstanding importance for the future. And of course, a further aspect was how best, strategically, to proceed in the dialogue between management and shareholders in a shareholder democracy to achieve the greatest media echo.

As a traditional, German, publicly-owned company with over 30,000 small shareholders, Dresdner Bank was forced to resort to special PR measures. Responsibility for this rested with the bank's own legal services department, which usually examines all the bank's activities in one banking year to determine what is to be presented to the annual general meeting. From the beginning, the majority felt it would be necessary to seek approval by the AGM of all the details of the agreement. In this way, management could demonstrate that the business policy orientation had largely been established so that the concept could be resolved once and for all – formally and absolutely democratically – and removed from the agenda. The nightmare scenario whereby some nationalistic forces might at the general meeting wage a populistic attack against the alliance and appeal to dormant resentments prompted them to provide extensive information on the legal and contractual provisions.

How was Dresdner to explain a concept of such wide-ranging ramifications to the average shareholder? It was decided that, to begin with, the convening notice to the ordinary general meeting on 14 May 1993 should contain a detailed description of the contents of the agreement. From that, the shareholders could themselves infer the scope and the significance of the project. To make the voting procedure as irreproachable, formally, as possible the bank decided, moreover, to hand over to each shareholder attending the general meeting a copy of the agreement with the complete wording in German.

This granting of maximum transparency at a time when public interest was greatest caused a tremendous commotion as an act of exemplary PR work towards the shareholders. Never before had shareholders been granted such deep insight into a future-oriented component of business policy when business policy developments were at their most critical point. This act instantaneously cast an altogether different light on the image of Dresdner's capital market policy.

In Paris – also in May 1993 – the meeting of the holders of *certificats d'investissement* (certificates with subscription rights on BNP shares to be issued later) was also treated to an abridged presentation of BNP's strategic alliance with Dresdner Bank, which the certificate holders noted with approval.

The sudden, complete disclosure of the cooperation agreement in May 1993, at the very moment the strategic alliance was born, made a significant contribution to the further development of the idealistic side of the partnership. The willingness of both parties to lay their cards on the table instead of playing the usual game of cat and mouse with the press and capital markets astonished the interested public in a way that made them think that players were at work here who were apparently completely sure of what they were doing. The public also expressed surprise at the fact that it was possible to make predictions of such detail about the future in a sector that was deemed volatile, and in which there was absolutely no legal 'copyright' in that rivals are free to copy innovations – no matter whose – overnight and with impunity.

The astonishing way in which the tidings of the cooperation were eagerly accepted by the public and the markets confirmed, moreover, the effectiveness of ideological perceptive patterns triggered by a sensational development. The ideological view always feeds on mythical control mechanisms of a partnership that takes place 'for an unlimited duration', on an 'all-embracing' basis, 'simultaneously' and 'universally'. The observer of such an epochal event, grateful for such details, demonstrates a surprising amount of understanding for the fact that it may take a decade to complete. What is important is the pleasing undertone of the news: that here at last are people who can be considered competent and forward-looking and who are capable of courageously overcoming obstacles to create something never seen before. Who would be so petty as to doubt the undertaking?

Symmetry of legal form

Considerable understanding was also shown by German observers for the fact that the status of BNP as a wholly state-owned bank at that time offered scant prospect that an integrated, joint business policy with a partner of a different legal form might be realized any time soon; and yet it was assumed that this situation would be remedied after a relatively short transition period. Until then, no one had any fears that the alliance might be misused as an 'extended arm' of the French government's economic ambitions.

Certain harbingers of a forthcoming company-law symmetry of both banks nevertheless seemed visible. The fact that the Bérégovoi government was for the time being unable, for political reasons, to change the French state's position as sole shareholder of BNP had caused elation in Germany to recede. Nevertheless, the French government succeeded in putting on a show of well-disposed consideration to the alliance by demonstratively bestowing high honours on the chairmen of Dresdner Bank's Supervisory Board and Board of Managing Directors. And in general, the view was spreading that privatizations in France would be resumed shortly after the parliamentary elections in 1994, as the election victory of Balladur (the former finance minister and leader of the opposition) was deemed a foregone conclusion.

Certainly, professional observers of the banking and stock market scene applauded the fact that after years of guessing, here were reliable indications of how, in connection with the integration of the European money and capital markets, one might one day imagine the integration of Europe's hopelessly fragmented banking industry.

Antitrust clearance for the alliance

Typical of the legal debate necessary in the early years of the Federal Republic of Germany in the 1950s is the status acquired by antitrust legislation as a young judicial discipline. What is more, this material was taken over almost in its entirety in the antitrust rules of the Treaty of Rome of 1956.

For the German companies at that time, dealings with the newly created antitrust laws and the almighty German Cartel Authority (BKA) in Berlin, which stuck its nose into all business sectors, were a learning process the like of which had never been seen before. It was not until Ludwig Erhard abolished all manner of tutelage of industry and trade through state planning and authorization procedures that an extensive scope for development was created which it was up to the companies concerned to structure under their own responsibility, while duly observing competition laws.

However, for the German legal experts trained with Roman law terminology, terms such as 'competition', 'relevant market' and 'abuse of a market-dominating position' were completely new concepts. In practice, though, they soon attained special importance since one of the foremost concerns of German captains of industry was to be on good terms with the Cartel Authority, much as merchants had sought to be with the Church in the Middle Ages.

Another occupational group at the heart of economic activity at that time were the bankers. However, they had little to do with the BKA because Germany's law-makers wanted at all costs to avoid conflict between two federal authorities. For this reason, the BKA quickly decided that the German Federal Banking Authority (BAKred) should perform the Cartel Authority's function in banking. Over the course of time, however, against the background of efforts to make more rational use of the German government's bureaucratic entities, the BKA assumed a certain degree of responsibility for banking in abuse control operations, while the BAKred retained responsibility for all forms of price fixing agreements in the banking industry. The BKA was also made responsible for the registration of agreements among banks designed to restrain competition. Above all, this included rationalization agreements and other circumstances which, through the use of technical innovations, necessitated cooperation among banks.

In practice, this meant that the legal services departments had to ensure that all circumstances that could have a lasting impact on their own company's structure were immediately reported to the BAKred and confirmed by it. Further measures subject to reporting requirements were banks' memberships in multilateral banking associations (cf. Chapter 1), which – despite their de facto harmlessness – had to be registered under the stringent antitrust laws as so-called international restraints on competition. Next, formal proceedings were held to 'relieve' these associations of their anti-competitive quality, but for a limited time only. The principle that prevailed was one of preventative control.

The subsequent vice-president of BAKred had given a detailed account of this practice to a conference in Salzburg in 1973, not without irony. He described the cooperation agreements of that time as basic agreements containing a collection of 'meaningful and interpretable truisms', which is to say 'wonderful declarations of intent that were very generally worded and in which a great deal is said about working together, which one meant to do for the good of the banking customer and for the trustworthiness of the business'. The object of such agreements, according to him, were:

- the assurance of mutual preference and preferential treatment in all sectors of banking operations
- the use of one's own branch network for the partner's customers
- cooperation in the sectors of office automation, data transmission and examination of the use of technology for international banking activities
- the reciprocal invitation to take part in international syndicate transactions
- the clarification of joint issues of operating technology
- the exchange of staff for training abroad
- joint market research and pursuit of openings for rationalization in customer services
- greater support to be given to certain companies operating in the partner countries
- joint support of multinational companies
- support for company links between the respective partner countries
- an obligation to consult the partner before taking over or establishing institutions or before expanding the foreign branch network
- the establishment of joint representative offices
- the rationalization of all business operations in certain areas
- the establishment of a steering or cooperation committee and, if need be, of sub-committees
- to grant one partner the right to object to one-sided expansion by the other
- to launch projects to develop joint information technology (IT) programmes for security custody business, shared settlement facilities to accelerate payments, and so on.

The antitrust procedure in Brussels

The general meeting of Dresdner's shareholders on 14 May 1993 gave its consent subject to the proviso that the outcome of the antitrust assessment by the EU Commission was favourable, which was common practice in Germany. As a precaution, antitrust exemption had been filed for on 27 January 1993. The fact that the procedure dragged on for over 3½ years, not giving legal effect to the alliance until 26 June 1996, may be explained by several reasons.

The delay was largely due to the considerable scope of the contractual rulings. The banks, following the advice of their legal experts, were anxious to have every conceivable precondition for joint business activities in the various sectors checked and arrangements thought up that might possibly be necessary during the ten-year exemption period. To this end, empirical data had to be furnished, along with data from comparable years and annual updates.

Surprisingly, the parties to the agreement were not really put out by the prolonged duration of the procedure. After all, the pending procedure, the outcome of which they did not wish to anticipate, provided a plausible excuse for not taking any action as regards the partnership. Any awkward questions from the press could be parried by claiming it was in the hands of the authorities in Brussels, allowing the banks to appear as if they were raring to go while a higher force was – unreasonably – holding them back. Neither was the conclusion that the matter in hand must be momentous, shedding an aura of commercial potency on the applicants, so very undesirable from the PR viewpoint; it served as a smokescreen for the true facts of the matter.

That the EU Commission should finally object to a certain provision in the agreement did not come as a surprise. This particular provision had been retained to generate support for the project at both banks, and to preserve a certain manoeuvrability in negotiations during the final stage of the procedure. The provision in question concerned the mutually agreed protection of the two domestic markets in that, for example, BNP would be permitted to enter into cooperation with another German bank only with Dresdner's express approval. In the opinion of the EU Commission, this could not in principle be tolerated in the interests of the single European market, although the Commission did concede that such a strict exclusivity was to be respected in certain cases to protect know-how and business secrets.

Reform of EU antitrust policy in 2001 and its implications for such a procedure today

With its White Book on the modernization of EC antitrust policy of April 1999 the EU Commission surprisingly suggested, in order to 'simplify and accelerate antitrust procedures', changing its stance away from the rigid prohibition of the horizontal competitive restrictions and the preventative notification and exemption requirements. These proposals have since become part of legislation. As a result, the principle of abuse control replaces the procedure of exemption. This means that companies are no longer required to submit notification of their planned projects. Instead, they are free to engage in their activities at their own discretion until a cartel authority ascertains anti-competitive conduct.

This development came too late to affect the alliance of BNP and Dresdner, and yet this example can be used to ask, and answer, the hypothetical question as to how the transnational alliance between BNP and Dresdner would have been assessed under present circumstances and what the effects of such an assessment would have been. In other words, what course would probably have been steered on the basis of such a legal position to achieve the goal of establishing joint foreign operations? Many things would no doubt have followed a different course or been done in a different chronological order had the banks not been required to subject themselves beforehand to the above antitrust procedure with its wide-ranging implications. The signals they sent would have been different: from the drafting of the agreement to the setting of priorities, objectively and in time, in the form of a mutually agreed timetable.

For if, when the agreement was being drawn up, the banks had not been advised by legal experts to cover every single conceivable aspect that might cause problems at some point in the ten-year period, the agreement would probably have been 80 per cent slimmer. The banks would not have contrived declarations of intent for every aspect that might conceivably arise and then inserted precautionary legal 'plugs'. Instead, they would have been at far greater pains not to show their hand to the competition, since there would have been no need whatsoever to publish the agreement, and at its full length at that.

In such a situation it is unlikely that anyone would have dreamed of solving the anticipated problems, and of facing the shareholders, with doctrinaire theories instead of descriptions of reality. Transnational progress in Europe is not to be produced with declarations of intent but by taking risks on one's own responsibility and through insight gained from experience. It would not have been possible for a 'pause in transmission' lasting several years to occur in a key phase, during which the first burst of enthusiasm can peter out quickly if real issues are avoided.

Thus, having braced itself for so long for the theory-laden EU antitrust procedure, the banks were wrongly blind to the fact that the experiment could only be successfully completed as a learning process during which they had to acquire empirical knowledge by collecting findings of their own. Subsequently, the banks would have been in a position to stimulate expectations, one after another, and fulfil them step by step, with the participation of an interested public all the way.

4

The Birth of the Shared Myth: The Possible Nucleus of a Shared Brand

What is myth?

Myth is a message which – visual or verbal – it appears may be gathered from a certain historical event and tends to take on a life of its own.

In contrast to primary-language statements, myth is not defined by the object of its message, but by the way in which it utters this message. Everything, then, can be a myth? Yes, I believe this, for the universe is infinitely fertile in suggestions.[1]

Myth as a semiological system

Semiology is concerned with the relationships between the signifier, the signified and signs, which together form an associative whole. The essence of myth is to allow the presence of the signified to shine through the signifier. In the realm of language the signifier is called 'meaning', in the realm of myth 'form'. Whereas the linguistic 'term' tends to be unequivocal, the 'sign' is ambiguous, just as the signifier of myth is ambiguous. True, it contains meaning and form, yet in an ambiguous form as a result of which the message appears somehow empty or unfocused, and myth then moves into this ambiguous, 'emptied' context. In so doing, it draws attention to itself on two accounts: one, it indicates something, and two, it implies something through which at some time the need for action may be suggested.

Power of motivation in myth

Myth hides nothing and shows nothing. Unlike ideology, myth does not deny things. Instead, the function of myth consists simply in talking about them. At most, it distorts them in that it changes primary-language forms in

27

its own way. Not every unclear situation produces a myth. Often, the mythical message remains too dim to develop any kind of motivation, and just as often the message is too clear to be credible.

Forcefulness of myth

Myth emanates a power that is spontaneously convincing. In most cases its effect is greater than the rational explanations that are intended to refute it. Depending on what slant myth takes it can, through its suggestive strength, achieve anything or corrupt anything. Myth is a language that will not fade away. It gives things, according to their appearance, a natural clarity, not explaining but confirming. In this way, things give the impression of meaning something all on their own.

When reading a myth, it is not the authentic truth that counts but how the reader might gain a useful insight from it. The effect of myth cannot be perfected in terms of content: it exists as it is. Neither knowledge nor the course of time can change it as such, meaning they can neither add anything to it nor take anything from it. Since myth is a 'phenomenon of value', it is pointless to exercise influence on it by challenging it. It is to be got the better of, if at all, in a roundabout fashion by attacking the context of its message.

Myths as the driving force of economic activity

According to Eugen Böhler, economics is not a wholly rational thing or even a system of economic equations, but moves between two poles: between the irrational and rational, or between experience and concept, between wish and reality.[2] This means that the same person who behaves rationally as producer is irrational as consumer. Thus, if consumption becomes the main issue for him, it follows that irrationality is his actual driving force in acting economically.

His mind is increasingly steered by myths, the roots of which are primarily in spiritual needs that people have acquired in their dealings with one another. When fantasy comes into play – through rational representation – as the central force it gives the project in question the glamour of something of value, making it seem attractive as a result. Thus, it embodies the driving forces of an economic society, no matter how rationally they express themselves.

General mythical leading ideas and particular myths

Assuming the actual formation of value in trade and business takes place not so much in the factories as in the market, it becomes clear just how major an influence myths wield as an economic influencing factor. In their basic forms, a differentiation must be made between, on the one hand, the general leading ideas to which ordering functions are attributed in the competition of economic systems with each other, whereby they claim a general validity for their legitimization, and on the other, the indeterminable mass of particular myths to which are assigned the individual economic subjects whose fate in competition they share according to the ups and downs of opinion-forming on the markets.

Since the correctness of fundamental regulatory policy issues cannot be proved with scientific precision, their legitimization is based on consensus among the specialist faculties and on the democratic legitimacy of political bodies from whose statutory foundation they stem. The relative lack of focus of these leading ideas requires that in day-to-day politics, work is done constantly to improve them. That is why it is necessary that the social elites commit themselves wholeheartedly to their unlimited legitimization from which, in turn, their political nimbus will result.

Typical of particular myths is their unquenchable thirst for greater and greater prestige. All economic subjects need this prestige, as it is representative of their position on the market and their prospects of being able to maintain or strengthen their position.

The following may be said for both categories of myth: myth is vital because it is, on the one hand, an expression of hope. On the other, however, myth is blind because it has to ensure our survival notwithstanding the misgivings of common sense and science. For this reason it simply blanks these areas out. Thus, myth is the cornerstone of all our human actions and, consequently, also of economic life.

Media as midwife and mouthpiece of myths

By dint of their private-law autonomy, the media take it upon themselves to concern themselves virtually full-time – either by commenting on them or by expanding upon them for promotional purposes – with particular myths in that they try to create, amplify or oppose them. The professional makers of myths behave as if they had embarked upon a mission in the field of public opinion-forming on behalf of civic society, whereas in fact their sole concern is usually to stupefy, to stun, or even to shock with eccentric statements. With their amalgam of fact and fiction, and their prime objective of entertaining and of providing information, the media are the ideal setting for the formation and spreading of myths.

Ever since the works of Marshall McLuhan[3] were published in the 1960s, it has been well known how little these media are concerned with conveying objective messages. Instead, their purpose is the presentation of their own wondrous nature. If need be, they will casually refer to recognized achievements of other media and so participate in their legitimization. This being the case, if media are to have any chance whatsoever of reaching their audience they must work constantly to astonish with surprises and exaggerations. To put it crudely, they live by hyping things up.

Of artificial myths and 'organic self-acting processes'

Myths emerge or are born in one of two ways: they are either artificially stage-directed, or are spontaneous and without preparation. The former category is the rule, which is obvious if only for the reason that an influential business sector devotes itself to the task and never ceases to tell us so at every turn in our everyday lives.

One does not have to tot up the budgets spent by businesses on advertising and PR to realize how vastly important it is for companies to work on their own myth, given that each company's myth, as a necessary 'calling card' in the consciousness of the public, plays a dual role as intermediary and as standard of comparison. Wholly different are the effects that a 'natural born' myth produces spontaneously, which are not stage-managed or manipulated; they are born out of an original occasion or situation, within a significant context. Such a myth's meteoric entrance on the stage of contemporary consciousness produces among its recipients a heightened interest in the onward development of this phenomenon, and opens up promising options for its continuation.

Both forms differ, then, in terms of how they come about and what effect they have, which is to say in terms of the depth and durability of their effectiveness. Speaking metaphorically, one could compare it to the difference between a puppet theatre and a theatre with actors of flesh and blood. Although the artistic achievement of the former can be considerable, its effectiveness is not to be compared with that of the stars on the stage. For the moment the puppeteer gives up business, the life of the puppet is extinguished, whereas a famous actor remains what he is, even when a show closes for lack of funds.

It is quite simply a fact that the public considers a spontaneous, unadulterated myth credible and more attractive. Compared with such a myth, the half-life of an artificial product that has emerged from the calculated strategy of advertising experts is usually a matter of only weeks or days. If it is not artificially resuscitated it expires, and its place is taken by another myth.

Myth as a loyal brand follower and unswerving devotee

Just as a creation demonstrates affection and gratitude to its creator, so a myth behaves towards its actual starting point. This is to say that as long as it is alive, it showers unshakeable loyalty and adoring ardour upon it as its idol. Like devoted admirers, followers afford themselves the luxury of believing in the boundless success of their beloved club, star or any other extraordinary phenomenon. The advantageous and disadvantageous characteristics of a myth – or of a follower or fan – are as shown below.

PROS	CONS
• care-free	• unteachable
• optimistic	• opinionated
• cosmopolitan	• insistent
• hungry for action	• exaggerating
• steadfastly encouraging	• stubborn
• absolutely devoted	

Since myth is in essence a 'phenomenon of value', it is futile to seek to exert influence on it by questioning the reason for its enthusiasm. The Achilles' heel is the constancy of its idol, which is expected to stay the same (that is to say, it will not change).

Existence of a shared myth as a competitive advantage

Anyone fortunate enough to have such an effective intermediary *vis-à-vis* a broad public ought to be clear about how this asset *sui generis* is used to achieve maximum benefit, both externally and internally.

Internally, too, it can perform considerably integration work as a shared 'servant and guardian', provided it is handled in a circumspect manner. If endeavours to convey consistency internally are successful, this can in turn prove beneficial to work done externally. A credible correspondence of both aspects can, against the background of what is happening elsewhere, arouse an impression of an effective development, and so contribute towards the strengthening of the myth.

'Brands': myths 'hardened' in the fire of competition

That brands as 'corporate brands' are synonymous with the further development of myths in the commercial field is already implied in their definition.[4] According to this definition, brands are imaginary images in the minds of the consumers, the purpose of which is to serve identification and differentiation. Such images relevant to products and services are stored in our brains as brands. Brand leadership is all about transferring brand identities to the market in such a way as to make them visible. Strong brands stand squarely on two pillars: brand recognition and brand image. Being frequently confronted with a brand makes that brand more engaging, increases confidence in that brand and encourages the consumer to give preference to it.

The decisive challenge to brand management lies therefore in establishing clear brand identities. A successful brand has a profile, just as a human individual does, which is rationally comprehensible as brand use and central competence. Somewhat irrational factors that come into play are the inner world of emotions and images, personal disposition with regard to personality traits and the self-images of potential customer groups.

The establishing and heightening of existing brands are among the key tasks of business management. These are, as investments in intangible assets, just as important for companies as investments in plant and factories are in production. Through brand extension the attractiveness of an already existing brand is extended specifically to new products, which may by all means serve to strengthen the basic brand. Brand management is a matter for the top executive level, and is considered too major an issue to be delegated.

Cross-border banking alliance as a media sensation

As has been said, what the authors of the cooperation agreement were aiming at was sympathy advertising by issuing the agreement in the form of a manifesto addressed to the shareholders, the capital markets, the EU Commission as antitrust authority and, more generally, to public opinion in Europe.

In the process, the vague intention of creating broad-based curiosity about the arrival of something new by making unclear statements surprisingly hit the bull's eye.

The unexpected, complete disclosure of the cooperation in May 1993 also, as has been said above, played a part in this success. The decision by both parties to forgo the usual game of hide-and-seek with the press and capital markets and, instead, to surprise by demonstrating openness was right on target. The interested public was impressed to note that it was possible to make such highly detailed forecasts in such a daring undertaking in the services industry.

However, the stupefying effect is not to be explained by this strategy alone. Why this act proved an unprecedented surprise was probably also due to the fact that hardly anyone in banking would have thought this particular duo capable of playing a leading role in an internationalization drive of such dimensions. What's that? This ingenious concept, set down in a differentiated agreement, has already cleared the hurdles of supervisory boards and their 'attorney generals'? Intense preparatory work must have taken place, hidden from the prying eyes of the world press. Hats off to them, if that is all true!

Yet even the admiration for intense preparatory work and the discretion with which the work was done does not fully explain the stupefying effect. This was probably also the result of the terrible realization on the part of market observers that the new order in the international sector, which they had always called for, was actually already much further advanced than had been assumed. Had developments really progressed so far that predictions of this kind were possible?

The eagerness with which the public, the capital markets and the media received the message of the possibility of transnational cooperation was indeed a surprise. A self-igniting process had taken place, and it struck like lightning. Seen from the mythological angle, the hazy, unclear categories such as 'of an unlimited duration', 'all-embracing' and a 'simultaneous' and 'universal' cooperation, more than anything else, are what proved in terms of the myth to have a particularly stimulating effect on the recipients' imagination.

A dedicated follower, moreover, is always ready to forgive his idol imperfections. Who, then, would be so petty where matters of such significance were concerned? This applies, for example, to the speed with which this message was accepted. The consumer heard only the underlying tone of the news to the effect that, finally, competent and daring people had ventured to overcome age-old obstacles to achieve something the likes of which had never been seen before. And suddenly, the traditional misgivings about supposed economic policy asymmetries – which is to say the fact that BNP's status as a 100 percent state-owned bank held out little prospect of achieving an integrated, joint business policy with a partner bank from relatively liberalistic Germany – caused little concern. Previously voiced Cassandra calls, to the effect that Dresdner would be abused as the 'extended arm' for the French government's economic ambitions, were forgotten.

Nevertheless, the asymmetry of the legal status of the two banks did manage to make itself felt. The zeal with which the Bérégovie government denied rumours of forthcoming privatization plans heightened the impression among observers that once the 1994 parliamentary elections were over, the resumption of privatizations could be expected, with that of BNP top of the list.

Thus, Dresdner and BNP at first made very sparing use of the strategic alliance topic for PR purposes. This reserve was noted very favourably. Here is the reason why the image of the two partner banks underwent a complete change, both in the market and in the press, within a short period of time.

Advance praise for the 'Franco–German duo'

Expert observers from the banking and stock market sector welcomed the fact that after years of guessing, reliable indications were finally being offered as to what form a close dovetailing of the European money and capital markets would take. This mood was reflected in May 1995, when the European dailies surprised their readers by reporting that Sarrazin and Pébereau had been voted European Bankers of the Year. A group of 21 business journalists chose the alliance members for a newly created award with which the financial centre of Frankfurt am Main had sought to draw attention to itself. The *Handelsblatt* of 15 May 1995 had this to say:

> By voting the duo – Jürgen Sarrazin and Michel Pébereau – 'European Bankers of the Year', the group of 21 from the Main has expressed their confidence in the joint future of Europe. For Dresdner Bank and Banque Nationale de Paris (BNP) have, with their extensive cooperation agreement, taken a forward-looking path towards a partner-based German–Franco cooperation the likes of which has not been seen before.

Long-term objective to establish a shared 'brand'

Looking back at what has been said regarding the myth, the question arises as to the logical, tangible objective of such a development. We have seen how in the initial phase the partners succeeded in producing a spontaneously igniting myth which not only built a bridge between two national cultural circles and two national economies but also gave rise to hopes of the emergence of international banking communities. Assuming the logical consequence of this development is to establish a shared brand, it follows that new structures might arise across national borders as a result.

If brands of banking groups instead of only individual companies are what count at international level, competition in this sector could become more transparent. In particular the newly emerging, extended banking markets could profit from such a development as the rigid borders of national banking industries would be loosened and, at the same time, cross-border stability created.

Whether the initial success of a shared myth is sufficient for worldwide operating corporate brands to emerge which will cover as many areas of international competition as possible must be doubted under the present circumstances. Nevertheless, BNP and Dresdner succeeded in highlighting the prerequisites for a possible future development of this kind.

To follow a path with such an objective in mind, however, calls for singleness of purpose to the last. If one considers the multi-layered influences to which a large European bank is subject, day after day, at national level alone, and which must invariably affect the alliance as well, it must be considered extremely doubtful that it will be possible to overcome, indefinitely, these multifarious hurdles. Not least, what this requires is the innovative strength to follow a new path and, above all, financial staying power. The experiment will quickly run out of steam if fuelled only by short-term improvisations. All that will then remain is a failed project which sets a negative precedent highly capable of hampering further developments in this direction.

Finally, if the task at hand is to be mastered, one must possess the ability not to overestimate the importance of initial success by standing still. This means that further steps have to be taken, ceaselessly, to consolidate what has been achieved, and to build upon the shared myth with the ultimate aim of establishing a shared corporate brand as a symbol of new paths in competition.

Notes

1. R. Barthes, *Mythologies*, translated by Annette Lavers (New York: Hill & Wang, 1984).
2. E. Böhler, *Der Mythos in Wirtschaft und Wissenschaft* (Freiburg: Rombach, 1965) p. 149 *et seq.*
3. In particular M. McLuhan, *Understanding Media – The Extensions of Man* (Cambridge, MA and London: MIT Press, 1964).
4. F. R. Esch, *Strategie und Technik der Markenführung* (Munich: Vahlen-Verlag, 2002) and *Frankfurter Allgemeine Zeitung*, no. 71 (25 March 2002).

5
Obstacles and Hindrances on the Way to the Transnational Alliance

We have seen that a cross-border strategic alliance is not to be realized in one great leap, but that it is conceivable only progressively as a self-realizing process. Limitations are set for a process of this kind in that it has to be aimed in a certain direction, meaning in this case a global partnership for conducting banking activities in third countries. In principle, however, it is a development of unlimited duration. In light of this, the cooperation agreement emphasizes the need to achieve individual solutions step by step according to the local circumstances in each case.

If – unlike the European process of political unification – no binding time-table is given, it is appropriate to ask after more than a decade why the expected development did not take place. To be more precise, the question of greatest interest is: to what phase did the process actually advance, and why did it not go beyond that stage?

Seven phases of the progressively self-realizing strategy

There are seven phases involved in this, as shown below:

- agreement on the global strategic objectives
- breakdown of the global objectives by fields, sectors and geographical areas
- identification of concrete projects, localization of the joint bases and specification of the expansion phases
- feasibility studies for the relevant projects with regard to marketing, technology and the economic environment
- putting together the teams and function-specific preparations
- budgeting of the relevant projects
- evaluation of controlling reports.

To anticipate the outcome straight away, it may be said that apart from two exceptions that will be discussed below, the global process of the alliance never aspired to progress beyond the second phase. The question, of course, is why this should be. For the most part, the reason quite simply lies in the nature of the beast.

Unstable contributions to the alliance by executives 'on loan' from the partner banks

To assure the alliance of the necessary basic leadership skills in foreign business during the difficult start-up phase without running up excessively high costs, the partners agreed to delegate, on a parity basis, members of their middle management to participate in meetings once every quarter. There was no alternative to this approach. The task would have been impossible for anyone from outside the alliance. Not only would he or she have needed to know both languages and both banking cultures, but that person would have had to be familiar with the decision-making channels at both big banks; in other words, to have known who is well-disposed towards and who is opposed to the alliance, who has authority and influence, and so on.

Consequently, it seemed far more appropriate to entrust experienced middle managers with this challenging task. Besides the quarterly meetings to be held between specialists from one bank and their counterparts from the other, important matters were also to be discussed and resolved on an informal, ad hoc basis.

Bearing in mind that these bankers had to perform important functions and duties in daily operations as well as sit on strategic committees to decide on the concretization of objectives of the alliance, the question arises whether this – pragmatically-driven – combination of different duties to be fulfilled by managers with an already packed schedule was indeed so beneficial for the alliance.

In retrospect, it has to be said that because of the different group-dynamic situations during the euphoric initial stage and thereafter, as well as the diverging standpoints involved, this compact solution for dealing with alliance-relevant topics did not prove itself in practice. If, for example, it was necessary to exchange information on daily operations and give both sides an opportunity to think about specific forms of application in the joint business activities in certain regions, it made sense to hold back until the strategic framework of the alliance had been formulated. On the other hand, daily operations were, strategically speaking, an indispensable field for experiments that would provide more exact information on what operations warranted development.

Nevertheless, it remains obvious that strategy – notwithstanding opportunities existing in daily operations at the time – must dictate the framework that specific business realizations are gradually designed to exploit. If this framework is transfigured externally by an impressive goal, there is a good chance, despite all the adversities in daily operations, that this prophecy will be fulfilled as part of a self-realizing process.

The euphoria fades

In spite of this, after the alliance received the go-ahead from the general meetings of shareholders in May 1993, an order was issued for the implementation of the cooperation to be started straight away, provided the effects were of a purely internal nature for the time being. Thus, although the necessary strategic framework had not yet been established, the cooperation was already under way. Purely for reasons of economy, however, quarterly meetings of the strategy committee were planned to coincide with consultations on daily operations.

One fact proved to be fatal for the alliance project: within both bank hierarchies there was only a very thin layer of foreign business experts who possessed the specialist knowledge that allowed them to make decisions regarding the shaping of the alliance, the means of implementing the joint strategy and the acceptable risks in daily operations, not to mention the costs involved for the partners. In one case, decisions might be needed in connection with basic questions of architecture and the long-term objectives of the alliance, and in the next it might be the strict evaluation of specific transactions according to the professional criteria of the respective partner banks.

The principle of separating responsibility for strategy on the one hand from operations on the other – a matter of course even at companies operating nationally – is even more strongly called for in a cross-border alliance that is just getting started. If these two responsibilities are mixed, the decisions made on the operations side, besides being often far more pressing, automatically assume the character of test cases for and against the feasibility of the transnational alliance. In other words, the psychological pressure which a series of negative decisions in operations is bound to produce will inevitably raise the level of frustration at both banks. This would poison the openness and vision that can characterize the medium- and long-term strategic parameters. At the very least, it demands the ability to abstract from current developments.

It is not surprising, then, that as discussions on the meaning and the purpose of the alliance grew less and less clear, more and more bankers expressed the opinion in private that it might be better to call the whole show off before the confusion and the damaging effects of a growing disorientation got any worse.

The blurring of the different functions within the alliance had a further, questionable effect. The intention of creating, with the strategic alliance, a constructive climate for a merger project between two large banks at a later point in time was vanishing by degrees. How could the partners have kept this option alive? As a result of their specific training, the bankers in each country were not in a position to come up with adequate answers. They had been trained only to follow clear, and clearly explained, instructions. Even the managers delegated to the strategic committees were not prepared for the task of developing with their counterparts from the partner bank a new, separate strategy that hinged upon cooperating with partners from a different, a foreign bank.

The typical bank executive was not up to a challenge that implied such a far-reaching delegation of responsibility. Within a large bank, executives must be able to adapt to and subordinate themselves to the given strategic orientation. Thus, the individual who had worked to acquire the requisite conformity of thinking was not necessarily the uninhibited innovator needed to get such a revolutionary concept up and running with relatively little in the way of instructions or directions. When have executives been allowed the freedom to shape policy themselves?

The fact is that such far-reaching strategic decisions called for the charismatic authority of the most senior executive level of each bank. Indeed, this could only be two people. (More will be said in this connection in the next chapter.) The natural consequence of the calamity was that the overtaxed delegates thought it appropriate to divest themselves of their responsibility by delegating it back – albeit bashfully – to their superiors.

However, the bosses of the two banks could not allow orders to be delegated back to them. The strategic alliance was supposed to be borne on a broad basis by middle management. Consequently, there would be a certain lack of strategic clarity for an indefinite period of time. The top men at the partner institutions initially chose to see their main task as providing suggestions as to the general development the alliance should follow. As a result, the next steps of concretization of the strategic objectives remained vague and schematic. The charisma of the banks' two top men was what it would have taken to give clear contours to, and put flesh on the bones of, the alliance concept.

Moreover, the initial euphoria had the effect of largely ignoring the harsh reality. But the more reality finally moved into full view, the more the second and third management levels, who had assumed their tasks relevant to the alliance subject to the proviso that the necessary inspiration would come from the 'creators' of the partnership agreement, felt they had been left in the lurch. The outcome was that objectives still could not be concretized, which in turn cast a poor light on the plausibility of the strategic alliance as such, particularly during the difficult start-up phase.

Fear of crossing the threshold on all sides and at all levels

Allowing the strategic alliance to unroll as a self-realizing process with an open end may seem a particularly flexible approach. The more thoughtful members of staff who eyed the long, uncharted stretch of the road ahead had their misgivings, however, and their numbers rose steadily. Were they really up to the job, or had the banks greatly overestimated their own powers in subscribing to this heart-stirring vision?

The effect of the fear of crossing the threshold, regardless of the level at which it strikes, takes the form of a mental distance that suddenly arises *vis-à-vis* the emotional state of happiness caused by the myth of the cooperation. The myth succeeded masterfully in painting the transnational alliance in the most brilliant colours as an epochal 'first' and referring to the 'tempting prospects of success' at the end of the process. But the moment this suggestive power loses its force, a cool, defensive reaction takes its place and the actual situation is analysed with a remarkable degree of clarity and decisiveness which gives the impression it had never been assessed any other way.

Thus the fear of crossing the threshold, which takes control at this moment, activates – like a 'warning system' from the subconscious – the collective self-preservation tendencies of one group. The fear of crossing the threshold performs, one might say, the function of 'border guard'. It is part and parcel of the basic anthropological make-up of ethnic groups and acts as a kind of self-restriction which contributes to the avoidance of conflict with the outside world on a lasting basis.

Proceeding from the above, when one permanently exposes oneself abroad by relocating the main focus of one's sphere of activity to another country, a hitherto neglected inner voice makes itself heard to warn against taking potentially self-destructive risks. The inexorable effect of this inner anathema usually kicks in the moment irreversible commitments are entered into, which is to say the moment permanent investments with a built-in risk of loss are made beyond the national border.

As a company approaches this point, little remains of the initial mood of expectancy. Suddenly, all that counts are the possible successes it is about to give up on the home market. This reflex, therefore, does not hinge on one's impression of the partner, but is a consequence of the fearful contemplation of the part of the 'adventure' that lies beyond the 'protection' of the national border. Voices can almost be heard to cry: 'Are we really so hard up? We still have a couple of aces to play on our home market that offer potential for expansion. Should we not reconsider after all?'

Reactions of this kind are not an expression of national arrogance but rather, above all, of sudden despair at the hardships the shadowy part of the road ahead has in store, after initial euphoria had made success seem absolutely attainable: the view through the mythical veil that had hitherto surrounded the objective. Suddenly outlines appear of something altogether different from the original image.

6
Alliance of the Augurs as Jointly Acting Brand Leaders

After reading the previous chapter the reader may be wondering how it was possible for two prestigious companies in the banking industry, both of them among the 20 largest banking groups in Europe, to go public with such an auspicious project that had no time restriction, when not even the second phase out of a total of seven had been successfully completed. Seen from a mono-causal, analytical view, such a procedure appears somewhat problematic. On the other hand, considering the limited extent to which such a test criterion can claim to cover the field of reality in question, it would hardly be possible to derive from it a generally valid mode of procedure.

For example, if one takes myth as a relevant factor, a totally different picture presents itself. From the end of the first phase onwards, this factor can make an important contribution to the outcome. This will be looked at more closely in this chapter with regard to its mythologically versed tamers, figures who hark back to a tradition-steeped institution that asserted itself for over 900 years in Ancient Rome: the augurs.

We saw in Chapter 4 to what (scarcely overestimable) extent myths are the true driving force behind economic life, since without their forward-thrusting, optimistic influence our economic life would – because of various points of friction and exaggerated precautionary measures – suffer from endless stagnation, and many developments that appear to us to be indispensable would not take place. Consequently, success according to our current conceptions is realizable only if reality is 'taken in tow' by strong myths: that is, if myth – more or less coordinated – gives wings to reality and propels it forward.

Only when a convincing myth 'strikes up' do participants in economic life really prick up their ears and listen. Put another way, from this moment on no one has any interest in theoretical definitions of the type gathered in the final six phases because 'grey theories' are quite simply ignored by the economic subjects as boring.

Seen from this angle, the cooperating partners did well to go public with the project upon ending the first phase, to test whether a sustainable myth might be coaxed out of the cooperative approach chosen, for that is what they needed to secure the customers' approval for this venture.

Chapter 4 looked in detail at how a myth comes about. It originates as if by magic from vagueness and meaningless patches of primary-language textures as metalinguistic information which takes on a life of its own and calls forth a series of illusions and motivations in the consciousness of contemporaries. These, in turn, give rise to certain actions and, as a consequence, very specific developments. Further, we have seen that in business most participants are at pains to create myths synthetically and launch them according to a carefully directed strategy. As a rule, these attempts run out of steam very quickly despite the exorbitant advertising budgets spent on them, and vanish. The only exceptions are 'organic' or 'naturally grown' myths, and these must be considered a stroke of luck. For this reason, their systematic exploitation as 'assets' can hardly be thought of too highly. Such a myth is the magician who 'makes the puppets dance'. It is his favour that must be won and maintained.

Shared myth as the core of a transnational relationship

What has been said about the emergence of myth makes clear that myth in its specific forms latches on to, and subsequently sticks with, a specific cultural context. Only very rarely is it powerful enough to leap beyond the confines of this specific cultural (in most cases, national) context and establish itself in foreign climes. This being so, myths are limited to certain national modes of perception in a way that jokes also are. To put it crudely, myths are rather chauvinistic spirits who stir the imagination of insiders, usually leaving the outsider (foreigner) cold.

In this respect, the question as to the existence of transnationally valid references is the same as the question of whether there are also myths of a superlinguistic kind, which are capable of fascinating, as it were, a number of different nations. At a trivial level, phenomena of this kind seem to be much rarer, yet it is on this level that the transnational cooperation myth that emerged within the scope of the alliance between BNP and Dresdner Bank is to be considered. This, in turn, seems possible only in connection with the personality of its inventors and animators.

Of course, the way the two cooperating banks issued simultaneously a message of the same content to their national and international public goes a long way towards explaining why a transnational myth came into existence. What was also necessary in this context was that convincing representatives had come up with this idea. The duo of Jacques-Henry Wahl (BNP) and Jürgen Sarrazin (Dresdner Bank), the initiators of the alliance, were without doubt convincing representatives who at that time exerted a decisive influence on the business policy of their respective banks – particularly towards the international market – and so created a high degree of credibility for the idea of the partnership.

These two leaders embodied, each in his own way, the shared concept. Each expressed himself in his own style, and yet both were able to give listeners the impression that they had thought the concept through, in mutual agreement, to the end. Thus, both were able to give any information that was needed. Together both were, one might say, the guarantors of the feasibility of the concept. Their employees and the press responded to the generous measure of charismatic authority both men possessed with almost boundless faith (an important foundation for a myth in the making).

The style of both individuals did have something in common, but only as the bottom line. Neither of them would tolerate problems being dramatized. Wahl, always with a joke at the ready, was a master listener; with an arch smile he would encourage speakers to think further about the issue at hand, only for them to discover there was no problem after all. Sarrazin, feared for his 'elephant's memory' and his powers of precise deduction, excelled in detecting the error in reasoning behind an alleged problem. This, incidentally, may well be why hardly anyone at Dresdner dared to speak his mind about the purpose of the partnership. Only remarks vouched for by the master himself were repeated and passed on.

Given the character sketches of these two wise men of the alliance, it is understandable why almost no one thought of consulting each of them individually if something was not clear, to compare the responses. Such was the confidence they conveyed, namely that a far-reaching consensus existed between the two leaders on the objectives and methods of the envisaged alliance, that nothing could really go wrong. No matter how often lower-level managers may have wondered, at meetings, if the other side really was pursuing the same goals, the knowledge that things were proceeding with complete conformity at board level was assurance enough, dispelling doubts that things were perhaps not so cleverly laid out at the solely authoritative level after all.

The above phenomenon is a perfect example of the strength of the shared myth as that of an 'all-embracing' instigator on a lonely road, who promises an elitist status to those who will go with him. Further propulsion is lent by the fact that below the 'wings of the shared plane', lifting forces make themselves felt, giving the pilots and situation analysts confirmation that they are on the right course with this subservient spirit, the cooperation myth. This is reason enough to say something about the augurs, their original task and their ascension to being chosen as the topmost executive authority.

Augurs of Antiquity, a mixture of shaman and top management

The charisma of the top men of the alliance and their exceptional intuition for the myth that had to be developed is reminiscent of the leading role played by the augurs of Ancient Rome. As a metaphor for an all-embracing, quasi-magical competence in interpreting extraordinary, historical developments, these figures must be given preference over that of the Indian guru because the augur has always – despite acting behind the scenes – represented an important share in power.

The constitutional mission and the status of the augurs are among the most impressive testimonies to Roman statecraft. This is true if only because this institution was never abolished in roughly 900 years of the evolution of the constitution. On the contrary, their function was upgraded under each reform until finally, in the last phase of the late god-emperorship, it was merged with the emperor's office, a union of *imperium* (means of command) and *auspicium* (privilege to make predictions in political or military affairs). In the time that followed, this concept was part of the inventory of traditions of the absolutist understanding of the state in Europe, which was regarded as the 'auspice' for everything and all things. To this day, no language can dispense with that meaningless, flowery phrase demanded by protocol: 'under the auspices of ...' *auspiciis regis* (higher judgement of the king) or *sous les auspices du Roi* (under the higher insight of his Majesty).

It is truly astonishing that the bearers of absolute military and police power were so intent on seizing this function for legitimization reasons. They obviously felt they could not do without their monopoly of the mediation of higher protection for the community.[1]

The cultivation and control of myth by augurs

As has been said above, there are limits to the extent to which the emergence of a myth can be controlled. From the moment something self-sustaining starts to develop, the beneficiaries should be sure to nurture and support it.

The augurs' task of lending support to the myth and of coaxing it, by cunning and trickery, in the right direction is essentially a matter of finding the right mix of measures needed, on the one hand, to animate and, on the other, to control. It is important to accommodate its speculative suggestions as far as possible inasmuch as this is in the customer's best interest. In short, myth must be given every opportunity to develop its attractive qualities to the full, to show itself from its creative and encouraging side.

On the other hand, it is vital to show it the limits that are necessary for it to maintain its sharp profile in the market. This entails keeping it 'on a tight rein' so as to prevent contradictory and unrealistic exaggerations.

It is important to keep tabs on the 'Achilles' heel' of the myth. As has been pointed out, it needs to be seen to be identical to its original starting point. Thus, its special effectiveness lies in its originality, in its being faithful to its 'trademark'. For example, if it gains a reputation for always being good for a surprise it can allow itself extreme behaviour, whereas that might be irritating with another type of myth, and its image would appear 'blurred' as a result. All its life the myth is dependent on the perceivable existence of its factual starting situation, which has become the cornerstone of its image.

If, then, it were to take its antics too far there is a risk that the myth's starting situation may have to be seriously corrected by its guardians and controllers. This would mean a loss of its convincing power and vitality, causing its effectiveness to suffer in the long run. The foremost concern of the myth's minders, therefore, is, on the one hand, to do everything to make the myth appear as balanced as possible, to prevent it from conveying impressions of being chaotic; and, on the other, to maintain the topicality of the starting situation in a credible manner, and above all else to avoid making fundamental changes to it. If the augurs succeed in keeping their eye on these points, the public will be relatively trusting in that they will not be interested in details of specific activities. Charismatic authority arouses global confidence that everything will be handled properly.

By maintaining these general expectations of charismatic leader-types it is possible to respond more intensively to specific charms of the myth: for example, to devote more attention to local moods in customer behaviour and to keep the requisite elements of surprise at the ready. If at any time there is a break in continuity, immediate steps must be taken to create a plausible substitute situation, as then there is the possibility that a suitable replacement myth will immediately succeed it. The public should be given the opportunity to react according to the saying: 'Le roi est mort, vive le roi!' (The king is dead, Long live the king). The question as to any qualitative differences compared with the predecessor is to be played down as far as possible. Only in this way can a maximum of the prestige and attractiveness of the first myth be salvaged and passed on to the successor.

The transnational cooperation myth in particular

We have seen that a strong, natural-grown myth that has securely placed itself in the collective consciousness is a rare and valuable asset in the commercial sense, and it demands to be used intensively. Even more valuable, because it is even less common, is a transnational myth that has a factual basis that anchors itself to (and is virulent in) the collective consciousness of two nations.

This factual basis, which has to be 'legible' in a number of ways, acts as it were as a hinge between two national markets. In this particular case the factual basis of the bi-national cooperation myth, which – internally and externally – is carried by a broad interest among the public, is the joint concept that the two augurs seem to have. This particular myth has the makings of durability provided its foundation is properly cultivated and systematically developed by both parties.

As an enthusiastic fan capable of great devotion, the myth derives a great deal of satisfaction from such a constellation. It seeks the proximity of its idols, one of the two augurs, and is gratified when they fully agree with each other and bestow a smile upon it. This is the proof that the world is in order, that things are proceeding in the right direction, and the myth expressly congratulates itself on this. It can do nothing but lavish 'ovations' upon the object of its admiration. This does not go unseen by colleagues and neighbours, and encourages them to join in. In this way, the perfect starting point can be created for the sales situation.

Such a convincing factual basis would, of course, do well to ensure that the existence of cross-border forms of cooperation is made apparent at as many locations as possible. This is why, in 1993, the order was issued that within the scope of the alliance all existing challenges were henceforth, without a supraordinated time schedule, to be tackled everywhere. The intention here was to take from those further down the chain of command the excuse that their particular sector was still waiting to be officially included in the partnership.

On the other hand, one can easily imagine that to follow this general order without a prioritized, target-oriented coordination would quickly result in considerable confusion. This is precisely what happened, as Chapter 8 will reveal.

Note

1. Definition: 'augur' means authority to determine the will – if any – of the gods in reference to the success or failure of a specific undertaking by the state or military, in two ways: (a) usually by prophecy (auspices or augurs), as a message of the gods in the form of a sign; or (b) in exceptional cases, after the fact as an interpretation of sudden phenomena (as a spontaneous expression of the will of the gods). Case (b) most clearly reflects the legal power and authority of the augurs. They could call for the immediate postponement of any public assembly by announcing that the signs were unfavourable. Moreover, the college of the augurs could determine by resolution that disturbing auspices had occurred, for which reason a certain act of state was (according to the rules of their science) flawed and consequently had to be reversed.

   Authority to ask for auspices is solely the privilege of the top constitutional bodies: the right to request auspices is part and parcel of the most senior echelon of power (*imperium*); those so authorized include the senate, public assemblies, magistrates and official priests. Thus, only the most senior constitutional bodies were entitled to have their auspices consulted (meaning the praetors, for example, but not the propraetors).

   At first the college comprised four members, then six, and from about 300 BC there were nine. From Sulla onwards, the college had 15 members. The members were appointed (for life!), and the right to fill vacancies rested with the college itself (cooptation). In the Late Republic (Sulla onwards) it rested with the people. Finally, in the late autocratic period, the prerogative to appoint new members was that of the emperor, who made the mediation of the help of the gods a sign of his absolute power.

7
Strategic Alliance: Preliminary Stage or Ultimate Objective?

Are prospects of a possible, later merger the true object of the alliance?

When, in 1989/90, the two institutions had agreed on the alliance they faced a dilemma over how they should explain the purpose of their surprising joint undertaking. Initially they agreed quite simply and sensibly that this strategic alliance was in fact just an interim phase during which the partners could size each other up and weigh up the envisaged joint business activities. If the alliance were to prove itself the partners would have to approach the owners of the two banks in due course to recommend their merger.

Mutual contractual obligation to keep the option of a merger open

Although roughly 90 per cent of the cooperation agreement consists of non-binding standardized declarations of intent in which the partners set out in generalized form their 'pious' intentions, a number of specific undertakings are to be found which involve refraining from – rather than doing – something. The aim of these undertakings was to prevent a merger of both companies on equal terms from being watered down by subsequent actions of either party. These include the undertaking not to acquire more than 10 per cent of the partner bank's shares on the stock exchange (Section 4.2). Similarly, jointly held participations were not to be disposed of without the other partner's express consent (Section 10.1). And finally, no substantial agreements were to be entered into with a rival from the partner's home country without the other's express approval (Section 6.2).

All three provisions are self-evident, and were intended to prevent one partner from carelessly snubbing the other (or, to put it another way, to keep the partner's prestige intact).

This is confirmation that the long-term intentions of both parties went in the direction of a cross-border merger, since it was not considered out of the question that cross-border mergers might one day be the norm as a truly European banking market materialized. In that case, it would naturally be a tremendous advantage to have already secured a suitable and strong partner for such a merger, and to be able to point to results already generated through close cooperation with that partner.

Another opinion was that the realization of an extensive strategic alliance was the real sensation that deserved to be duly publicized, for if two partners already complement each other so well at a cross-border level, they could conceivably – not least given their infinitely greater flexibility – achieve more than some hastily cobbled-together merger which involved making hurried arrangements that would have to hold for a long time to come. Thus, if the main point of the exercise is to shape the strategic alliance on a global scale, the project must be laid out in such a way that the tasks to be accomplished may be approached in a consistent, steady manner, one step at a time. The public, the natural sounding board for the shared myth, would certainly have gone along with that, and willingly so, even praising it as proof of the expertise that was at work.

With regard to the time factor in implementing the concept, there was really no reason for rushing to release the unfinished concept on the market. There was no sign of direct competitors in this particular sector; indeed, there are none to this day. Had the two partners taken more time they would have been better able, above all, to handle the difficult twin task of joint foreign operations on the one hand and the complexities of business at national level (where signs of a sea-change, at least in the initial phase, were becoming apparent) on the other.

Further, in placing too heavy an emphasis on the evolutive process, the partners should surely have realized they would eventually walk into a trap of their own making: in other words, that they were unnecessarily stoking doubts as to whether the efforts made really were capable of achieving the ultimate goal, for the risk of failing to achieve the goal can, ultimately, never be completely ruled out. A fundamental doubt that grows with time is bound to do substantial damage to the credibility of the entire undertaking, given that market observers are never slow to address difficulties the moment they crop up.

The main concern, however, was to point out to customers immediately that the two partners had something sensational to offer. With regard, in particular, to the press it was essential that they take notice of the innovative nature of the joint undertaking as soon as possible. This made it essential, under all circumstances, that the leading formers of public opinion did not show merely a limited interest when confronted with a vague label such as 'interim phase' or 'provisional measure'. In other words, on no account must a reaction be provoked from the media along the lines of: 'Just look at the work that still has to be done! Come back later once you know what you really want.' If only for this reason, the strategic alliance had to be heralded from the outset as *the* great improvement.

All this thinking about how best to present the alliance to the public did not alter the fact that the alliance was, for the circle of colleagues closest to the augurs, an attempt to position their own banks ahead of others on the road to the new age of a European banking industry. The supposition here was that big banks created by a bi-national merger would have a pioneering role to play. Since the two banks agreed so closely on the project, they felt it essential – if only for reasons of time – to act according to the saying: 'First come, first served'.

Three questions of feasibility as a prerequisite for a promising start

A methodically correct procedure would have required that the augurs sufficiently examine in advance the feasibility of three questions before giving the go-ahead for a cross-border strategic alliance. This would have been necessary if only to be able to take the wind out of disbelievers' sails by saying: 'We have well-founded evidence that the goals we have set ourselves are, in principle, realizable. What's more, we have made enough risk venture capital available to finance the job.' These three questions may be summed up as follows:

1 Under what conditions are transnational myths conceivable in the mercantile sector, given the cultural barriers within a Europe consisting of rigorously separated international forms of consciousness?
2 Can it be taken for granted that the European consumer of banking services is interested in foreign services and products while shunning the tried and trusted services offered locally?
3 What resources, qualitative and quantitative, will both partners be in a position to employ in the foreseeable future to realize the achievement and usefulness potentials needed to tackle this gigantic task at an international level without encountering resistance from the partners' own shareholders?

It would be right to object that this short catalogue of questions, too, is still very general and that greater differentiation is needed with regard to the achievement and usefulness potentials according to sectors, divisions, currencies and local traditions. Justified though this objection is, however, it does not negate the necessity of finding the answers in good time.

In actual fact, however, these questions were never clarified. Faced with the unique constellation in world politics at that time, immediately after the end of the Cold War, it was suddenly decided that this project should remain confidential no longer. Trusting that the time was ripe, the banks no longer wanted to withhold the message the public had secretly been waiting for. As we have already seen, the response was completely in line with what the banks had expected. The myth was assembled in double-quick time and demanded, above all, to be fed with gripping details.

The big question, however, was what to feed it with. Since neither partner had a suitable pool of advanced concepts to draw from, hasty PR work was called for to still the hunger. The banks felt immensely flattered by the interest the press on both sides of the Rhine lavished upon them. Inside the four walls of the alliance, however, the banks had very little to offer. They were unable to provide details of how the vision was to be turned to reality, and neither did they see any possibility of changing this situation any time soon. Throughout the ranks, both banks were lost for answers. These could only come from the top.

Clearly, the assumption was that once they got going, the rest would somehow fall into place. It was surely no problem for a large, internationally experienced bank that commanded a leading position on its home turf and had many experts in the international field to fill in the gaps in the plan of action.

However, especially when an attractive and powerful myth is available and the timing of broadcasting its attractiveness is all-important, it is crucial to have a stock of forward-looking know-how to fall back on at the decisive moment. Where this is not the case, confusion and counterproductive action are bound to ensue. When no thought has been given to how visions should be given substance, second-guessing by a single person will not do any good, however much of a clairvoyant the individual might be.

Only the augurs acting in concert can lead the way out of such a tight corner. Though it was, strategically, the right approach to present the institution of a transnational banking alliance as a winner from the word go, rehearsals are necessary before a musical performance can be advertised. It is too late, after the announcement, to think about which composers might be asked to compose some pieces of music.

Seen from a vantage point ten years on, the boundless self-confidence of the two banks is astonishing. The feeling of omnipotence the internationally operating banks had at that time arose out of a certain myth, namely the way the global Eurodollar market and, related thereto, the global Eurobond market operated. Both markets were run by the banks autonomously through private-law agreements. For a long period dating back to the mid-1960s, it was to this myth that the world owed the financing of a worldwide boom. No wonder the banks were able to derive from this their proverbial 'power' in business, which in turn gave rise to expectations on the part of the public. Against this background the shared myth of BNP and Dresdner caused a stir because a strong tandem from the banking sector was thought capable of performing certain pioneering services in the process of European integration.

Was the alliance propelled by European integration?

Sarrazin gave an interview in June 1997,[1] two years after Dresdner, acting alone, acquired the London investment bank Kleinwort Benson; for a number of market observers, this was a demonstration of Dresdner's having distanced itself from the spirit of the alliance. Referring to the monetary developments seen in Europe in the meantime, Sarrazin had the following to say about the status of the alliance: 'From the beginning, this cooperation was geared to the long-term objective of growing together.' He and Pébereau had been in agreement, Sarrazin explained, although they both saw something different in the collaboration between BNP and Dresdner Bank in the longer term from what was then the status quo.

> Only, no one today is interested in 'long-term'. Everyone wants results straight away. But that's not what our cooperation – for all the positive things that may be said about it – was primarily designed for.
>
> If we had already made greater progress with regard to European integration when we signed the cooperation agreement, BNP and ourselves could today certainly present a more intensive form of Franco–German cooperation, of European cooperation.

Does the ultimate goal go as far as a merger? Sarrazin does not say this, but he does say that sometime in the future the cooperation between the two big banks will have taken on another form. 'If Europe develops the way I expect and consider desirable, one day both banks could by all means grow together.' A long way because, for this to happen, many things still have to be harmonized in Europe, first and foremost legal and tax aspects.

Certainly the alliance is no longer restricted to setting up joint subsidiaries in far-flung regions. Both institutions, says Sarrazin, are working on a joint payment system and on products that will come on to the market with the introduction of the new European currency. Yet such projects, Sarrazin concludes, are nothing that might be sold to spectacular effect.

These detailed remarks, made by Sarrazin at a relatively late stage of the alliance, are symptomatic of the partners' mindset, especially during the initial stage, and they primarily concern the role that was to have been played by European integration as a driving force for mergers rather than merely as a backdrop.

Upon closer inspection, what is to be gathered from his forthright remark: 'If we had already made greater progress with regard to European integration when we signed the cooperation agreement, BNP and ourselves could today certainly present a more intensive form of French-German cooperation, of European cooperation'? Behind it lies the idea that had integration been at a more advanced stage at that time, the process of the growing together of both banks would have happened virtually on its own. There would have been no need for more precise information on, say, the benefit to (and the preferences of) foreign customers. Of decisive importance was and is solely the impression made upon the press. If the impression is favourable, all that is necessary will have been achieved.

This is roughly the premise behind the notion of the transnational strategic alliance as a 'self-acting process'. Also astonishing is the claim that at that time it was not possible to gauge the trends of European integration. Market psychologists were already hard at work for hundreds of companies in Europe researching the preconditions for customer strategies. But the banks believed they possessed superior insight into what the realities were and had no need for such instruments. Not until the mid-1990s did Dresdner start making use of demoscopy (population research on opinion polls). Had the two partners already done so then, they would have learned how hard it is to sell banking products across cultural borders. In particular, they would have been able to appreciate the obstacles that present themselves in cross-border customer services (see Part II).

What does this mistake tell us about the initial premise of the joint undertaking? That it obviously is not a self-acting process, a sure-fire success, and never will be? What is to be said of the undertaking as such? It would be best to call the whole thing off? The only answer that would save face for the time being was to carry on: 'We keep going until one day we have the wind of European integration at our backs and we can prove our theory of the "self-acting process".'

Advanced stage of European integration as a precondition for cross-border, private-sector initiatives

Sarrazin correctly points out that a banking initiative really only makes sense if intra-European relations in the goods sector, above all between Germany and France, are sufficiently advanced.

Certainly, a stronger growing together of the markets could have further enhanced the nimbus of European integration and generally invigorated the business climate, impacting also the banking sector. But would this have triggered a specific demand for cross-border banking services? Normal growth could have been handled using the traditional instruments available to national banking industries. The question that remains, therefore, is: what would have been evidence of a more intensive European integration in the private business sector? And the disappointing conclusion also remains that, contrary to all promises, this development had deceived somewhere along the way.

Indeed one must agree with Sarrazin's remark to the effect that, from the 1990s, European integration did not spark any appreciable growth in direct intra-European trade compared with the previous three decades. There were, of course, cases of growth, but these were indirect in nature in that they were booked in the accounts of the distribution companies that had been specially set up in neighbouring countries, before being transferred to the parent companies, and thus no new organizational processes were created as a result. Consequently, the manner in which European integration presented itself in the private business sector was virtually unchanged. This explains why, contrary to expectations at BNP and Dresdner Bank, there were no notable increases in Franco–German customer relationships. The prerequisites for spectacular innovation in distribution channels for cross-border banking services were therefore not met. The assumed calculations for such new sales channels had been disproved by this reality, prompting the two banks to scale back their cross-border experiments to more of a 'business as usual' level, and to review the objectives of the alliance. This makes it understandable that the partners, having reached this decision, saw no need to engage in any far-reaching studies on the special sociological implications of a transnational banking alliance.

Asymmetries between European integration at the political and at the private business level

The public both in Germany and in France still found it difficult to swallow the idea of state-owned banks being part of any cross-border linkages of banks within the context of European integration. After all, BNP at that time held a certain key position in France's state-supported foreign business activities. This jarred with the private-sector myth of a large bank in Germany, giving rise to the question whether the shared myth of the alliance might not suffer permanent damage as a result.

Bearing in mind what has already been said about the two categories of myth, we may detect a rough division into, on the one hand, the general system-supporting myths attributed to humankind as such and, on the other, the universe of private-business sector phenomena. Myths in the form of universally valid value orders in state and society have also included, since the Second World War, the European communities and their legislative European integration programmes as prominent examples. Hovering about this formation is a multitude of sparkling private-sector myths, all of which endeavour swiftly to attract attention to themselves in the mercantile sector by offering smart solutions in order to gain the consumers' benevolent interest for as long as possible, and that not only in the national markets.

The difference between both categories is almost as vast as that between the gods of Antiquity and the common mortals. This is why a leading state-owned bank of a leading EU member state did not fit into the picture. Fortunately, privatization had long put paid to the irritation this caused. The simple point to be made here is that the false categorization into these two groups might lead to false conclusions when appraising the prospects of a strategic alliance, for market observers interpreted this situation in such a way that a state-owned bank should be seen as having a place among the gods given its limitless possibilities; this fuelled expectations of 'show-biz razzmatazz' and expansion.[2]

A considerable asymmetry can be seen to exist between the above two categories when assessing questions of the business policy opportunity of subsidies. Whereas political parties and government bodies are constrained by aspects of democratic legitimacy, which is to be underpinned by election results, opportunity in the private sector can never stray from the calculatory and other business policy targets with impunity. Hence the dogma that only such activities may legitimately be engaged in as justify the expectation that they not only pull their own weight in terms of costs but also generate profits to finance further expansion and preserve their capital stock.

Thus, for reasons of opportunity, political parties and government bodies can as a general principle subsidize certain social initiatives that are close to their hearts and which will be opposed, if worst comes to worst, by certain minorities of the public. The above dogma virtually ties private-enterprise initiatives to their calculatory targets.[3]

A private company which, on top of the above requirements, is bound at all times to the special disclosure requirements that listed companies have to meet is in a totally different situation. If it loses its earning power, for whatever reason, its energetic basis (and, with it, the radiance of its myth) can in a worst-case scenario be extinguished. Its star in the private-sector firmament immediately grows dim; its existence becomes a problem the moment market observers suspect a connection with unorthodox corporate objectives.

How does the myth of a large bank see itself? The track record of the French and German banks over the past 120 years has been equally impressive in terms of safeguarding the existence of their respective national industries through times of change. This gave rise, in the minds of investors, to myths that had the radiance of a comet's tail, and left all sense of reality far behind. Ultimately they, too, are destined to fade.

Journalists may find it appealing to call to mind the history of these time-honoured institutions and to prevail upon them thus: 'You must start playing the role to which you were born, namely that of midwife to a transnational European economy. To this end you must equip yourselves with organizational forms that are state-of-the-art worldwide. It's your duty to help something new establish itself at a transnational European level! The time is ripe to make a fresh start as we bid farewell to the Cold War! Thanks to a partner with global presence, a partner so well suited to you, it should be possible to demonstrate to others just what a "Franco–German motor" can achieve.'

Fuelled by suggestions of this kind, the shared myth of the cooperation shifted, unsurprisingly, into top gear. It proceeded to impress everyone except those who, as augurs at work behind the scenes, were well aware of the weaknesses and pitfalls of such a challenge. Theirs was the difficult task of bringing these lofty ideas back to earth, back to reality. This involved picking from the long list of expectations placed in the shared myth certain (organizationally feasible) projects that were within a safe range, and to realize them without overtaxing the capacities that were actually available.

Notes

1. *Frankfurter Allgemeine Zeitung*, no. 124 (2 June 1997).
2. The curse that dogged the nationalization of French banks in 1982 was that cunning minds believed more benefit could be gained for the French economy by dint of this difference.
3. This being so, three years after BNP was privatized, one can envisage Sarrazin and Pébereau, who incidentally worked harmoniously with one another, as two figures tied to one another (metaphorically speaking) and endeavouring stoically to abide by the private-sector laws under which they had taken on their task.

8

From a Global Spectacle to a Focused Joint Servicing of Customers

After the cooperation agreement was passed by the shareholders' meetings in May 1993, the augurs announced that henceforth the gradual implementation of the agreed cooperation was to be started at all levels wherever points of contact between the partner banks presented themselves. Commissions with an equal membership from both banks set about their work, meeting alternately in Paris and Frankfurt. Dialogue developed, for the most part by coincidence, at various functional levels. People who, just a short time before, had been somewhat incredulous to learn of the existence of their counterparts offered each other their products as if to say: 'If you haven't got this or that yet, just help yourself!' What an opportunity for mutual enrichment.

Unfortunately, upon closer inspection, the national product and marketing solutions in place at one bank appeared rather strange and did not slot easily into the other bank's set-up. In other words, a great many comments and suggestions were made without a hope of ever being systematically classified, far less put into practice.

Whereas the partners had previously hoped that a systematically managed process would produce epochal innovations, they now faced an amorphous and unstructured mass of contributions, the general context of which appeared to be extremely hazy. Gradually, the suspicion arose that the so-called realization of the cooperation was mere activism, without a defined starting point, without clear-cut objectives and without, moreover, workable management instruments.

It was pointed out to anyone who criticized these circumstances that the agreement contained ideas that had to be filled with life, that there was no progress without a certain dry spell during which new things gradually proved their worth. On the other hand, the agreement contained principles which – and this, too, became clear – were difficult to realize. For this reason, the partners tried to mask this shortcoming by symbolic gestures, and by making generalized commitments to progress. This gave the provisions of the agreement a certain cult status, rendering the possibilities of an object- ive dialogue more limited than ever. Over the course of time, realization became more and more delayed, until an air of procrastination hung over the whole affair. The promised 'bottom-up' growth process, too, lost more and more credibility.

It was downright naive to assume that 'product specialists' who had previ- ously been accustomed to taking their bearings from clearly defined objectives within the framework of their national systems would saddle themselves with responsibility for a cooperation that was to proceed according to the 'bottom-up' principle.

Little by little the augurs, who never missed an opportunity to justify their joint course, showed themselves to be at a loss as to how the partners were to proceed in future. But just as the strategic alliance became progressively less of a 'self-acting process', with no chance of initiatives assuming concrete form 'from the bottom up', so it became clear that the alliance needed a radically fresh start that would have to include a change in methodology.

Purpose of the alliance: a cult community the partners served together, or a shared instrument to allow both to improve their business?

The purpose of the alliance was to be seen as giving both parties the oppor- tunity to achieve, by pooling their resources, an increase in performance which, had each partner gone it alone, would have been possible only by accepting special risks and costs. If this is made the foremost criterion, it is important to identify the acute deficits the partner organizations have in foreign business and to introduce the cooperation as the solution to the problem. To this end it is enough, initially, to address suggestions from daily operations within the context of the cooperation.

Thus the goal was no longer to perfect an idealistically conceived, abstract system the uncertainties of which were causing an ever-greater headache. To begin with, it was sufficient to embark upon certain projects that were geared to specific customer needs and to consistently develop and refine these by way of gradual planning, coupled with precise budgets and control of results.

It was probably also this change in methodology that caused the augurs to withdraw increasingly to their designated role within a dualistic management structure which was divided into the 'Commission' (the second management level which acted as the executive) and the 'Regular Meetings' (the top man- agement level of the partner banks). They became increasingly content with making visionary appeals to the creativity and responsibility of the delegated persons prior to meetings of the Commission. Regrettably their ideas were not discussed, with the result that their appeals were passed on, verbatim, to the subordinate levels, where they were placed on file without comment.

Cooperation as an empirical search process

The purpose of a search process is to identify productive areas of cooperation, referring to the respective organizational form. While conducting the process, more rational use is essentially made of synergy potentials – thereby enhancing competitiveness – by making bearable compromises, such as an equal sharing of the costs involved: Area of cooperation = cooperable subject matter + staff proficiency/willingness + adequate organizational alignment.

A new cooperation methodology made two other things clear.

1 The issue is not one of giving the alliance an organizational status in its own right in regions where one partner is already active (by setting up special operative units there under the banner of the alliance).
2 Any misgivings that the cooperation was bound to have the effect of restricting competition were rebuffed by the fact that the opportunity effects in competition varied widely for each partner, depending on location and field of operation, so that agreements of a certain duration made little sense from the outset.

Great expectations were placed on the Commission as motivator. This regulatory body of the cooperation comprised particularly influential members of the second management level at both banks, and was meant to give the alliance greater prestige and authority within the partner organizations. But this approach was flawed because such individuals were already heavily committed at their respective banks due to the key role they played there. This made it impossible for them to lay the foundations for what to them was a completely new (additional) function, at meetings scheduled to take place every quarter, without being able to become overly involved in the matters of the alliance between these meetings as their high position at their respective institutions demanded all their time and energy.

This point is demonstrated by the fact that more and more members of the Commission began to send lower-ranking colleagues to represent them at meetings, citing reasons of non-availability. Arrangements such as these were not envisaged under the alliance, and rendered even slighter than before the chance that they might familiarize themselves more closely with the special work the cooperation entailed.

Privatized BNP creates an opportunity to reshape the alliance

The French election in 1994 gave the right-wing/centre parties under Balladur a clear majority and – as had been promised – the privatization of nationalized companies was immediately placed on the political agenda. At the top of the list was the privatization of France's big banks, and in 1995

BNP was chosen to lead off after its earlier rival, Crédit Lyonnais, had apparently run into considerable difficulties.

BNP's prospects of success received a boost from the change of its Chief Executive Officer (CEO), with Michel Pébereau being appointed President/ General Manager. Pébereau had previously held the same position at Crédit Commercial de France, guiding that bank safely to privatization six years before. In the investors' eyes, therefore, his appointment was a guarantee that the expected placement of BNP would soon be a success, both on the national and on the international stock market. This assured BNP of a lightning start as a listed publicly held corporation and an outstanding position in the 'banks and insurers' stock exchange segment.

Given that the placement focused above all on the legal safeguarding of national investors' interests, the strategic alliance with Dresdner Bank was initially, of course, of secondary importance. But once the bank's international business policy had been mapped out anew, a large-scale re-definition of objectives and priorities in connection with the loss of a state-owned bank's privileges was unavoidable. This is to say that when foreign strategy was revised, the alliance with Dresdner had to be reviewed as well. Here was an opportunity to reconsider the usefulness of the alliance, to think about where and how the alliance might be given a new chance.

The organizational revamp of the alliance

After the members of the Commission had, as has been said above, practically 'deserted their post' by delegating their tasks – a measure not provided for in the cooperation agreement – the post-privatization structural reform at BNP provided a welcome opportunity to make some organizational changes. By dint of their authority, the augurs, without touching off further debate, declared that the mandate of the Commission (comprising between 12 and 20 members) was terminated and that successors were not envisaged.

At the same time, the augurs made clear that their semi-annual meetings – to be chaired by them and attended by alternating board members – would involve a worldwide stocktaking of the existing strategic plans with regard to the establishment of joint operative units and relevant investments. The implementation of these plans would be placed in the hands of special liaison people at the two banks' planning departments and human resources (HR) divisions. Extensive preparations were to be made on each item of the agenda for the half-yearly meetings to ensure that enough time remained to discuss the latest developments.

The ongoing monitoring of the joint ventures would be made the responsibility of the heads of the foreign development departments, who would make up the supervisory bodies at local level, with an equal number of members representing each bank. Many operational procedures were to be more precisely defined or replaced by simplified models. Further, there were to be no overhasty dogmatizations. The alliance was to retain its experimental nature. In the event that new developments did not prove worthwhile, structural adjustments would follow within a certain period of time.

The alliance makes a strategic about-turn

The augurs, then, jumped at the chance to agree, with a minimum of fuss, on a revised array of organizational instruments that were tailored to the needs of their personalized leadership. At the same time, despite the difference in business cultures, shared spheres of interest were to be more clearly set out. To this end, answers first had to be found to the following questions.

1 On what areas, and with what specific target, should the alliance concentrate in future?
2 What economic criteria and standards ought to be applied when selecting third countries as a target group for joint activities? (The aim here was to achieve greater relevance from the viewpoint of the two banks' business clients.)
3 Moreover, differentiated organizational forms were to be devised to boost the know-how of the alliance; what shape should they take?
4 Which continents or countries would be preferred, and what banking strategy measures would be implemented?

Departure from prioritization of global joint expansion

How did Alliance II differ from Alliance I? We have seen that the partners and overall content of the agreement remained the same. The change, therefore, was confined to a change of the augurs' concept: namely, to a concentration on the strengths of the alliance. This about-turn did indeed herald a completely new era for the alliance. Cooperation became more focused, more purposeful. Outwardly the alliance no longer served as the standard-bearer of a diffuse troop that sought to take the world by storm, but as a shared platform that would be chosen in certain cases to cater for the needs of the target group (the corporate customers of each partner bank).

In keeping with this new approach, the message was no longer the confirmation of virtual contemporary ideas, meaning the desire to attract attention by theoretical extravagances, but unspectacular work on specialized services that met the particular needs of French and German companies.

The descent from the 'Cloud 9' of the earlier shared myth inevitably ended in a hard landing into a world of intercultural absurdities in transnational business. However, the partners could only master such a change if the specific purposes of the reformed alliance were clear. For this reason, they agreed on the principle of focusing as the centrepiece of their new cooperation strategy.

From then on, what counted was no longer to deliver proof of an unspecified desire to expand together worldwide, but the will to concentrate on concrete services. Henceforth, everything would be geared pragmatically to the customers' needs, and the partners wanted to be just as open-minded about their objectives as the contracting partner at the other end of the deal. Differences in banking techniques and practices should always take a back seat. In future, it would be important to give customers the feeling that the alliance offered them an extended 'home'.

As from the end of 1995, conflicting PR excuses and empty promises of 'great solutions' to come became a thing of the past. It was time for the alliance to show its colours, to show how it would back up its claim that it played a leading role in the financial sector when it came to Franco–German initiatives and projects.

What focusing meant under Alliance II

In future, cooperation would take place only at the following levels.

1 Joint ventures (JVs) in new territory: challenges in what for both partners was new territory would be met by setting up joint units whose management would represent both partners on an equal basis. The central department for foreign planning at one partner bank would be in charge, as *banque de support*, of the preliminary organizational work. Future staff would undergo training in both national banking cultures for their respective duties. The integration of the countries of CEE into the western business world was, in the unanimous opinion of the customers and shareholders on both sides, just such a new territory *par excellence*.

2 Indirect presence in the partner's operational units by setting up a 'special desk': in the event that the foreign strategy of one partner did not envisage that bank's own presence in a certain category of country, the other partner having firmly established itself there, a special desk would be set up for the former if a brisk demand was to be expected. The employees seconded for this duty would be placed on the host partner's payroll and the earnings generated from this expansion of business would be retained by the host partner; the delegating partner would be content with cross-selling earnings made with the parent company in its own country. In this way, the subsidiaries profited from the ratings of their parents.

3 Franco–German cross-border business at domestic branch level: it was to become the task of sistered regional key centres in France and Germany to support Franco–German trade and develop talented individuals by means of on-the-job training.

4 Joint IT system developments and links: although national banking industries are effectively cut off from each other, and despite the restrictions this gives rise to, consideration was to be given to building bridges between IT systems which – in international cash management, for example – were intended to improve the interplay of industry and banks. National IT developments were to be simplified for transnational purposes to create additional opportunities for use in neighbouring countries. However, a critical mass of users in other European countries would be a prerequisite.

5 Intensification of the mutual provision of information: to ensure loan decisions in favour of subsidiaries of French or German companies in the neighbouring country were given a sounder basis and sped up, the relevant data were to be exchanged informally under a standardized procedure, the so-called cooperation loan, for the partner's confidential inspection.

Support to Franco–German customers in cross-border business

The servicing of foreign corporate customers by banks abroad has undergone vast changes over the last decades. Whereas the procurement of loans and finance for foreign companies in times of vigorous growth was still extremely difficult up to the mid-1970s, national governments set about wooing foreign investors from the 1980s onwards, and the banking sector played a key role in the brokering of development funds.

The big banks made a special effort to inform foreign investors about specific business customs and practices in the host country by training special corporate customer advisers, the message being: 'We have specialists who understand the hardships foreign companies face when doing business in our country.' However, it was only possible to offer these services in isolated cases as staff capacities were limited due to a lack of training opportunities abroad.

The reformed alliance of BNP and Dresdner Bank sought to remedy the situation by staff exchange programmes. Special empirical knowledge in Franco–German business was to be made the object of a special service. Obviously, the original intention was to cultivate a specially qualified and trained staff and to gradually set up organizational centres for them. The systematic expansion of these facilities was to be, as it were, proof of the efficiency of the reformed alliance as a trademark which ideally would once again buoy up the shared myth.

In other words, the more focused approach of Alliance II with its emphasis on bi-national corporate customer interests would, it was hoped, reinstate the shared myth with the Franco–German public as soon as results became tangible. Quite possibly the partner banks would have to scale back their expectations during the initial stage of the switch to Alliance II for, as has already been said, the suggestive effectiveness of a myth rises in proportion to the lack of clarity of its message. Fearing that the suggestive strength might be adversely affected, the augurs entered into a gentlemen's agreement to play down their change of course as much as possible. Now, they hoped to 'score points' by announcing that their intercultural expertise in bi-national business had been significantly heightened.

Obligation of loyalty to Myth I?

During the transitional period to the ever-growing Myth II, certain consideration still had to be given to the ongoing effect of the myth. Unfortunately, Dresdner Bank did not keep up its side of the bargain when, in 1997, it surprisingly decided to take over British merchant bank Kleinwort Benson, the international leader in equity business. Dresdner apparently saw this as an opportunity to expand its global equity operations. Much to the disappointment of the fans of the alliance, however, no cross-connection to the cooperation with BNP was envisaged, although it was clear that Alliance II had not provided for a focus on joint investment banking activities, which the disappointed commentators of the French press did not know. This being so, this step was in complete harmony with the gentlemen's agreement. The CEO at BNP had had knowledge of the deal from the beginning. BNP had consciously refrained from expressing towards its partner an interest in staking its own claim.[1]

Historical role models for Franco–German corporate banking services providers

A special service for French and German companies was already in existence elsewhere. For over 120 years, a banking group called Société Générale Alsacienne SA/Elsässische Bank AG with seats in Strasbourg and Cologne had been in operation. Its roots lay in the dramatic political fate of the bi-cultural population of Alsace-Lorraine.

The intercultural skills this banking group acquired on either side of the Franco–German border have maintained a high standard to the present day. After the Second World War, Banque Franco-Allemande SA, based in Paris and belonging to the Westdeutsche Landesbank's sphere of influence, gained a considerable reputation in this area. The above remarks may suffice to demonstrate the important pioneering work that had already been done in this Franco–German field of operation and which, as the EEC grew closer together, gave rise to prospects that demanded to be systematically perfected by a banking alliance on the basis of extensive branch networks.

This is why, from the mid-1970s onwards, BNP and Dresdner set about establishing more and more branches at the major regional centres of France and Germany, with a German desk in France and a French desk in Germany. As has been said, they were unable to acquire a sufficiently broad customer base. Consequently, from 1993 onwards, they were either dismantled or geared more heavily towards investment banking activities. This process lasted some three years. The caesura meant that a new approach had to be found, finally resulting in Alliance II, which made possible the systematic exchange of employees under the auspices of central HR divisions at a broad geographical level.

Realizations under Alliance II

When one considers the locations at which the partners set up joint offices within the scope of the revamped alliance, it is difficult to detect a consistent strategy or concept. First, the logic of the newly established foreign branches is to be understood only as a balancing of the existing foreign presences of both banks. These had to be set in relation to the current geographical preferences of both banks' corporate clientele. This dictated, as it were, the locations at which each partner wished to see its sales opportunities expanded through the alliance. Seen from this angle, each partner bank tried to have its respective network of foreign bases complemented as effectively as possible, namely at locations where it felt it was underrepresented.

For a better understanding of this starting point, a general historical comparison of both banks' foreign organizations would seem appropriate, for therein lies the key when appraising the branches which the banks had abroad and each bank's underlying foreign business philosophy.

Singular dimension of BNP's foreign presence

The differences in the foreign branch networks were indeed vast from the outset, a fact readily explained by historical circumstances. CNEP, one of the two predecessor institutions of BNP with a tradition going back over a century, had always seen itself as a global network of foreign trade banks to which a relatively compact domestic network with offices in the capital and at several industrial centres was attached. For example, CNEP had been the leading foreign address on the Australian continent from the very beginning, thanks to lavish backing from the French government as sole shareholder. As a systematic sponsor of national foreign trade, the French government was especially interested, in inflation-plagued times, in seeing the necessary clearing done locally, in foreign currency, through one of its own banking institutions.

Dresdner's historically-induced pent-up demand

The 100-year-old 'foreign career' of Dresdner Bank was quite different. As a universal bank that saw itself primarily as a securities bank, which is to say more of an investment bank, it engaged in commercial banking in more of a secondary sense in order to provide its corporate customers with a certain support. To this end it was enough, prior to the First World War, to be in touch with global capital market business through a branch in London. The rest of the bank's foreign business was routed through two domestic special-ized banks with a holding function, one for the Middle East and one for Latin America. After it was confiscated during the First World War, the London branch could not be revived, while the two domestic specialized banks lost a great deal of their foreign portfolio and saw their significance recede. Yet this did not mean any great loss in the time between the wars, as the frequent monetary crises and devaluations reduced foreign trade finance to a pitiful existence compared with the pre-war period.

What is more, foreign business, which was refinanced on a short-term basis in foreign currency, played a fateful part (and not only at Dresdner) from the end of the 1920s onwards. This explains the great restraint towards foreign banking exercised by Dresdner Bank's top executive, Karl Goetz, as temporary state commissioner and later as the long-serving chairman of the supervisory board. Throughout his life he believed that the greatest dangers to the development of the big banks came from abroad. As he remained in office until the early 1960s, it was not until the middle of that decade that Dresdner Bank was able to begin catching up with developments in the for-eign banking sector. First and foremost, this involved setting up branches abroad, whereby considerations of prestige took priority over considerations of cost and earnings.

When, from the 1980s onwards, Dresdner Bank switched more and more to correspondent banking to cut costs, the network of foreign branches grew substantially more slowly. Thought was given to a local presence only if German business interests were above average in the respective region. And when, soon afterwards, presence abroad became a favourite topic in Germany's financial press, the big banks saw this aspect as a central element of competition. They developed a fixation for the topic of which rival succeeded in establishing a branch office in which country first.

No wonder, then, that at some point Dresdner hit upon the idea of trying, jointly with BNP, to develop cost-saving models of operative foreign presence. Particular interest centred around the combined use of operative foreign offices that were compactly staffed and structured on the basis of complete parity, and where previously acquired inter-cultural experience in Franco-German banking would be brought into play.

Metaphorically, one might compare the foreign networks of BNP and Dresdner Bank to a heavyweight and a lightweight boxer meeting for a spar-ring session, but this does not mean it was not expedient to enter into an alliance as complementary partners. Nevertheless, the actual starting point did not correspond with the principle of absolute equality, a criterion the German bank deemed unalterable.[2]

Against this background, it is obvious why Dresdner was so interested in participating in BNP's 'riches'. Thanks to its extensive foreign branch network, BNP could afford to be present not only in the core countries of the mainstream strategy of international banking but also in a number of medium-sized and smaller countries in Europe. These countries, above-average benefactors of the growth of the single European market, were made additionally attractive by the comparative sparseness of competition, which translated into better margins.

Dresdner expressed interest in an indirect presence in three such countries, Belgium, Portugal and Greece, for which no operative presence was planned via BNP branches already in place there. A German desk would be established at each to cater explicitly to the needs of German companies, and a corporate customer specialist at Dresdner would be delegated to take charge of it. Since German companies make considerable use of the Belgian 'coordination centres' for foreign group managements in order to save taxes, all manner of corporate customers have set up bases there which are interested in the advisory and counselling services provided by a German bank. In Portugal, more than 200 German companies, most of them medium-sized firms, erected production plants in the 1980s, and there was constant demand for finance to expand them.[3]

Threshold countries the ideal target for joint venture activities

Countries with a vigorously growing national economy, in which no partner bank maintains a presence, make the ideal target for a JV subsidiary bank which constitutes, in the form of an integrated banking organization, a united French desk and German desk. For this reason, such a JV is an El Dorado for French and German companies because it offers more contacts with the host country than would separate operative units on their own.

In which threshold countries should such units be set up, one at a time, in line with the national corporate customers' needs? The symbiosis aspired to between the activities of the corporate customers and the banking alliance soon revealed that a formation of this kind can, at worst, go unnoticed within the context of mammoth economies. For this reason, every single partner has for decades been anxious to be perceived, especially in these countries, as a 'standard bearer' of their economy, and not as part of a piggyback formation with a foreign alliance partner. The opposite is true of medium-sized threshold-country economies with a population in double-digit millions, where alliance partners are keen to display a joint calling card, for, in such countries, a combined representation of interests is seen as an eye-catching innovation.

Of course, countries such as Brazil, Argentina and Mexico had attracted the attention of large European banks a good two decades before. As their economies improved on a sustained basis, European banks set their sights on other Latin American threshold countries. One good example here is Chile, where in 1996 the partners acquired a bank as a joint venture, along with a broker house. Other acquisitions in Latin America sadly remained confined to the realms of theory.

The states of central and eastern Europe: a magnet in the 1990s

After the exodus of industrial production from Europe to the tiger states of South-East Asia in the 1980s was interrupted in the mid-1990s by economic troubles in the Far East, European industrialists increasingly turned their attention to the states of central and eastern Europe where – for currency reasons if nothing else – signs of a dynamic economic trend were growing. One particular obstacle proved to be the state-capitalist mentality of the former state-trading countries on the other side of the former Iron Curtain. Ideological bridges had to be built to combat the inveterate anti-capitalistic mind-set. Only then could one hope to make direct investments from the West, although patience was needed on both sides to explain and inform.

The French partner, in its capacity as state-owned bank and in full agreement with the Quai d'Orsay (French Foreign Ministry) school of thinking, was the first to advocate the development of a banking intermediary role by setting up a local presence. Surprisingly, Dresdner went along with this suggestion, although for two years it had been busy deploying all available personnel and financial resources to help 17 million former East Germans catch up on 40 years of economic development as speedily as possible.

BNP and Dresdner quickly agreed that here was an epoch-making opportunity to prepare many roads for their own business customers, and not just in one direction either. This mission encouraged the augurs, Wahl and Sarrazin, to 'give their horses the spur' in order to tear them away from what was left of their operational units in Africa and Turkey, and to head them instead for eastern Europe at a gallop. As with trade with South-East Asia and Latin America, the aim of western companies was to translate gigantic wage cost and exchange rate advantages into competitive advantages in European trade. And another factor to be taken into account was that of transport. Compared with the 'antipodes' of the Far East, the central and eastern European countries were literally in western Europe's back yard.

What is more, Dresdner's joint market appearance with its French partner also offered an opportunity to shrug off national prejudices going back to the world wars, thanks to the high esteem in which French diplomacy was regarded in that region. Further, the combined offer of know-how from two different business cultures that were usually in a state of permanent rivalry refuted fears that one of the two cultures would endeavour with schoolmasterly insolence to invalidate the other. Whereas, during the initial phase, the alliance was still somewhat guarded on how, in practical terms, the cooperation would be expanded, it appeared from the customer's standpoint that the partner banks had now found a practice-oriented experimental field that would also make an ideal exercise ground with regard to organizational aspects.

The onus was now on the two central departments for foreign development to tap the potential of one east European nation after another, with one of the partner banks assuming in each case, as *banque de support*, and in accordance with its own methods, the organizational responsibility for establishing a bi-national presence that included the training of the designated staff members. The other partner would more or less play the role of passenger during the planning stage in that it would be party to everything without having to take the initiative. Instead, the other partner had merely to prepare itself for the coming local task and take care of what it expected would be the chief interests of its own customers.

It became evident that a bi-national team whose two members spurred each other on inevitably had to undergo certain learning processes. First, a joint methodology had to be agreed on as the partners gathered experience and progressively entered one country after another. Hungary was first, in 1990, followed by the Czech Republic in 1991. The number of joint ventures rose steadily to ten (see the list in Appendix 3 on page 147).

From the moment each JV opened its doors for business, all conceivable customer ties had to be activated via the competent branches back home and fed to the local teams. As this process was carried out absolutely simultaneously at the partner bank, the team members from different cultural backgrounds quickly drew closer together – as they did when it came to the fair assessment of the interests involved – and a working relationship based on mutual cooperation ensued. Of course, it was not always easy to hold one's own when faced with the authority of the *banque de support*, which always knew best what was to be done.

The true acid tests did not come until specific mistakes had to be corrected. In such cases, the French and German headquarters had to be notified and the culprits named. When this happened, both sides often raised highly ethnically coloured defences, necessitating top-level damage-restriction, and fast; not only the working atmosphere at local level but also the careers of the individuals concerned were at stake.

Nevertheless, western banks, acting as the vanguard for their corporate clients, faced a Herculean task. For one thing, the radical switch from state-capitalism to private enterprise meant that the central and eastern European countries needed wide-ranging constructive advice and practice-oriented training for specialist staff so that they could find their feet on the international business stage as quickly as possible.

Although the reforming states had a banking and financial system after a fashion, it had acted only as distributor within the closed circuit of the planned economy. It was not equipped, for example, to handle private payments from one bank to another. Clearing systems had to be initiated and the use of modern IT integrated, gradually, into financial and banking operations, and so on.

On the other hand, the business sectors of these countries had to be screened and production locations and labour market resources developed. Such exercises had to be geared to the criteria of prospective western investors, and so had to be made available in an appropriate form.

It is worth noting in this context the role to be played by BNP–Dresdner European Bank AG, the holding company opened in Vienna in 1999 to optimize the workflows and products of the JVs under the alliance.[4] This institution was also to be put in charge of units still to be established in central and eastern Europe. The experience gathered in individual countries would be pooled, evaluated for the benefit of colleagues in other reforming states to highlight similarities and foster the exchange of know-how, and systematically refined. These activities would also help to relieve the partner banks' central planning departments; this was a difficult undertaking because, although bureaucracies like to talk about having some of their workload taken from them, simply to hold on to their power they will not hear of themselves as being indispensable.

To sum up, it may be said that practical operations in the central and eastern European JVs under Alliance II were given a clear-cut profile through focus. Everyone knew why the alliance existed and where its locations were. Moreover, the partnership offered certain career opportunities depending on whether one wanted to bear responsibility for the alliance in a western or a central European country. But also in the Franco–German cross-border business at branch level, or in the jointly held specialist banks, it was possible to advance one's career by moving from one position to another. Alternatively, a banker who had been recruited by the partner bank as an expert for a certain period of time might later discover that thoughts of a 'return ticket' had been forgotten and that he wanted to stay put.

On the other hand, practical operations at the JVs were not immune to disenchantment, which sets in when the same criteria are applied to joint ventures as apply, say, to any other foreign shareholding. To have to live up to identical standards is as bitter an experience as for a spouse in a mixed marriage who is constantly reminded of the qualities of partners from the other's country of origin.

Methods of integrating the partnership more directly into the national branch networks

Under Alliance II, moreover, the efforts were stepped up to have companies for which business relations were to be established and expanded between France and Germany – across the cultural border – serviced by specially trained corporate customer advisers who were provided by both bank organizations. Their job was to give, like the German desk in the BNP branches of

Lisbon, Athens and Brussels, corporates from the neighbouring country finance-related assistance in setting up or expanding business relations across the border. This support was to cover not only special expertise in legal matters and business customs and practice but also intercultural communicative skills.

Five German centres for doing business in Germany, located at Frankfurt, Dusseldorf, Hamburg, Saarbrücken and Stuttgart, housed specially trained French colleagues to provide a highly specialized local service for French companies and their principal banks. In the same way, BNP sought out German corporate customer advisers versed in the French language and business culture for its branches in France to cater for the needs of German companies. These centres were located in the Paris region, Strasbourg and Metz.

These specially trained employees, who were normally assigned to the partner bank for a five-year stint, were the obvious on-the-spot contact persons for all the corporate customer advisers from the delegating bank. Yet by the same token they were experts within the new banking organization on questions concerning their native country, and they could also prove useful by accompanying colleagues on visits to customers.

The special quality of this network of experts in Franco–German business was that these bankers – ten in all – not only exchanged thoughts and ideas on an ongoing basis but that they could actually be contacted over the telephone by either group at any time when the need for specialist information arose. With time, a senior emerged on either side who was able, thanks to his expertise, to coordinate the various tasks and fields of activity. They also accepted requests for information of a more technical nature (for example, when, in connection with a loan for a subsidiary, the borrower's creditworthiness had to be based on the foreign parent's balance sheet situation).

Notes

1. This takeover unfortunately recalled an episode of BNP's history that was still fresh in the memory of the press. At the beginning of the 1990s, while still a state-owned bank, BNP had acquired a share of approximately 6 per cent in Kleinwort Benson with the aim of possibly bringing this participation into the alliance with Dresdner, where the partner banks would develop it together. But because Kleinwort Benson found itself in a temporary loss-making situation at the time, this idea fell on deaf ears at Dresdner. While reorienting its business strategy as a private publicly-owned company, BNP sold its share in Kleinwort Benson in 1995. Barely two years later, Dresdner was suddenly prepared to take over in its entirety a Kleinwort Benson that had recovered in the meantime. This episode did not add to the radiance of the partner banks' shared myth.
2. This probably explains why, in 1993, the Direction de Trésor as the top regulatory body of the French state-owned banks had great difficulty approving this alliance, which was to result in a 'super-holding' solution for the joint foreign subsidiaries with 50/50 ownership shares. But given that Crédit Lyonnais' single global player

strategy had already run into considerable difficulties, the regulatory authority finally agreed not to intervene in structural issues of the alliance so as not to disturb the experiment of a transnational banking alliance. Even then, however, it was apparent for a number of reasons that the super-holding solution would probably never materialize under a special contractual solution.

3. When the first German corporate banking specialist in Portugal prepared, after his agreed four-year stint, to make way for his German successor, the (French) head of the branch expressed misgivings about the cost of maintaining the German desk, and the experiment was consequently ended. The outgoing German was able to provide his own detailed accounts for the period of his activities. BNP accepted these as being correct and called for the experiment to be continued. By then, however, the staff member originally delegated was not available, and the model could not be continued after all. This brought BNP's head office into a precarious situation because it had failed to intervene in the decision by the local branch head as the person responsible for cost management there. Dresdner's interest in expanding upon this model was dealt a severe blow by this incident, and it was virtually discontinued. This shows just how thin-skinned partners in a transnational alliance can be (the sensitivity threshold is much lower than in national business) and how on account of their particular characters minor causes can quickly have far-reaching consequences.

Moreover, this case illustrates what drastic consequences the lack of understanding of each other's corporate governance and their management philosophy can have. The German bank, which would never have left such a decision to a local branch manager (if only because of the overriding significance of that decision to the alliance as a whole), at once assumed the branch manager's opinion was merely a pretext to conceal the fact that BNP no longer wanted to continue this model.

The French side, which attaches great importance to the unlimited responsibility of the local Directeur Générale, claimed it was unable to reverse the decision. Interference from the higher echelons of the bank would otherwise have been interpreted as an encroachment upon his responsibility for the bank's performance, BNP said, and would in this case have spelt the end of the strict cost discipline within the group as a whole.

4. According to J. Bachèlerie, a former secretary of the partnership who came from BNP, the great disadvantage of the new strategic formula, compared with a single banking group's natural foreign network, was that the individual JVs – even though successfully growing – had each developed an entirely different profile. The lack of homogeneity made it pratically impossible to form a common culture within a genuine common network which was desperately needed for the systematic development of human resources from a long-run perspective. While intensive contacts with the parent banks continued to exist, it was unavoidable that in some cases the two corporate cultures of the parent companies would sometimes extend into the common outlets.

For this reason, the idea of establishing a special holding company, located in Vienna, was finally adopted. The objective was precisely to encourage and to supervise the relevant JVs in order to give them the qualities of a truly common network. This regional holding company was planned to facilitate the control of the JVs by shortening the decision making process and to let them thus find their proper common corporate culture. See *Les Cahiers*, No. 9 (September 1998), p. 50.

9
The Will to Cooperate: Expression of an Intercultural Work Ethic

What does teamwork mean in the intercultural context?

Whereas the work ethic of earlier times was supposed to help the working individual find his personal value in the quality of his work, the modern-day work ethic concentrates simply on the term 'teamwork'. This includes, for example, sensitive behaviour towards others as well as other soft skills such as being a good listener, being able to cooperate in the broadest sense of the word and a collective adaptability on the team's part to changing circumstances. Surely no one would want to question this basic social consensus, and yet American sociologist Richard Sennett[1] believes that this generally prevailing understanding of teamwork embodies a sphere of 'demeaning superficiality' that casts its shadow over the entire working world. Sennett argues that, on entering this world, the individual leaves the realm of the tragedy in her struggle for self-realization to become part of a farce – for life.

Inter-cultural teamwork involves the ability to penetrate other cultures at any time in order to be able to evaluate matters across national borders. The processing of new experiences of reality and absurd situations forces the individual to strive for a degree of truthfulness that has little in common with the above 'superficiality' within a company. When an individual has to integrate himself into a team whose members come from different cultural backgrounds he acts as an inter-cultural bridge-builder. Merely running with the team is not enough to perform this task; skills in the high art of improvisation are essential.

In this constellation of constantly changing perspectives and situations, it is a particular challenge for the person in charge of an inter-cultural team to filter from the staff's different ways of perception a unique image with the help of which joint tasks can be tackled with the requisite creativity.

It is therefore hardly surprising that specialist literature on the Franco–German dialogue in economic life already fills entire shelves. A methodical self-criticism or criticism from the outside with regard to the occurrence of typical misunderstandings appears to be vital. Clearly it is worth consulting these works of inter-cultural research on a regular basis or studying them at training seminars. Of decisive importance is the ability to 'read' the 'signatures' of other cultures so as to be able to understand what they are expressing.

What does cooperation call for?

First of all, it is important to remind oneself constantly of how one's own company came to be where it stands today, its competence and its limitations in the face of domestic competition. Then one must learn to develop an empathic feel for the special orientation of the partner. This involves trying to find out where the partner's strengths and weaknesses lie in order to trace its rise from the nether regions of its domestic competitive environment to the heights of international competitiveness.

In this context, it is essential to adhere faithfully to a certain canon of deep-rooted priorities, preferences and methods based on IT systems and a certain methodology for gauging success. A qualified standard of performance thus acquired automatically expresses itself in a special feeling for one's own value. A clear remark to the effect that 'Our way of banking is best!', if made 'with a nod and a wink', will let a colleague know how serious a professional attitude is, and of any possibilities for compromise. Normative rules that are set up for reasons of safety are, in principle, not subject to negotiation.

The main thing to bear in mind when entering into an alliance is that each partner bank exists primarily within the medium of all-out competition. Seen in this light, racing to constantly raise performance is as natural as drawing breath. As with sport, the fundamental lesson one learns is that partners can only expect to realize prospects of success if they are exposed to a tense competitive climate.

To take, as an example, a cycle race in which the cyclists compete as individuals and in teams, it may be seen that such a climate involves competition both in the collective and in the individual sense. In a cycle race the participants have to spur each other on by constantly raising their own performance and, if one or more fall behind, joint efforts to catch up with the leaders must be all the greater. On the other hand, in the final stage of the race, the best-placed member of the team must at some point leave the other team-mates behind to realize – also in the interests of the team – her chances of winning.

The prime rule for coherence is: the more an alliance is pre-occupied with itself, the less competitive it must be considered, for the possibilities that exist of becoming preoccupied with oneself, and of becoming irritated and unproductive in the process, are many.

Irritation caused by the notional premise of an equality principle

Here the agreement contains one key error in logic. This is because it stipulates that every active measure taken within the scope of the alliance is restricted by the notion of equality of status in every single phase, a notion that reveals a not inconsiderable degree of self-doubt on the part of the partners. This idea comes very close to the idea of equality in syndicalism, which the small-minded find so plausible. The result is that when the partners at first see no guarantee that all the contributions to be made will be equal, they sulkily give up. Why? Because, clearly, unequal conditions are being demanded, which proves that the whole affair is no longer legitimate and it therefore no longer entails a commitment.

How, then, should one interpret the following sentence in Section 1.1. of the cooperation agreement (Appendix 1): 'Therefore BNP and Dresdner enter into the cooperation as equal partners with absolute and sustained parity'? This sentence establishing what is required from each partner seemingly demonstrates the importance to be given to notions of equality when embarking on a joint undertaking (hence the constant fear of being put at an unfair advantage).

This leads us to a further, fatal flaw in reasoning, namely the popular idea that partnerships amount to a 'zero sum game' as far as internal cooperation is concerned. This notion is fatal because it clouds not only the outside assessment by the partner but also the conception of oneself. It implies a constant projection to the effect that the contribution made by one party is constantly to be portrayed as above standard and that of the other – *eo ipso* (the move) – as below standard or inferior from the beginning.

It is therefore no surprise to see a defensive strategy adopted at central departments of the partner banks the moment a minor sacrifice is required in the name of the alliance. The question then asked is: 'Why us? Surely it's the other's turn now!', and so on; or else the procedure requested is dismissed out of hand as if to say: 'Isn't that just typical of the whole business!'

Had the above provision been more appropriately worded, it would have read something like: The main reason partners form an alliance is that they complement one another. Each party to the alliance has special characteristics and potentials that the other does not have to the same extent. Thus, the contributions cannot be equal in the sense that they are the same. On the other hand, all contributions are of the same or equal value inasmuch as they are appropriate as means of fostering joint success. It may remain open whether this refers to conditions at the start of the alliance, with regard to the employment of funds, or in connection with future performance. It is not the rigid 50/50 mentality that is the determining factor in the competitive environment but the market, which confronts competitors with changing and, consequently, unequal conditions. Certainly, such an obsession with equality reveals that the parties have an uneasy relationship with reality.

Whoever stipulates equality of status from the first lets it be known that he gives preference to an equal share of previously planned transactions over the alternative of being defencelessly exposed to a no-holds-barred competitive situation. In his opinion, it is better to hold on to what he believes is safe, placing little hope in unexpected opportunities that may be presented by joining forces. This explains the widespread practice of clinging to the 'my customer, your customer' mentality when it would have been far more appropriate to share responsibility for 'our customer'.

One could argue that such remarks about the equality obsession and the zero sum game attitude are general social-psychological phenomena that are just as likely to occur at a national as at an international level. While this is undoubtedly true, at an international level these phenomena are augmented by others (which will be examined in the following chapters) and consequently have far more disastrous implications interculturally than intra-culturally.

'Premeditated breaking points' in connection with contractual exoneration clauses

As a matter of fact, the partners toyed with the idea, right at the start of negotiations over the agreement, of leaving themselves a 'back-door exit' in the event that certain expected developments occurred or failed to occur. The line of reasoning was probably that they could spare their own self-esteem and put the blame for separating on the partner. Yet this would have amounted to an admission that they were themselves not in a position to keep the alliance from failing. Instead, they would rather risk a loss of prestige over the joint project.

In reality, instead of 'back doors' and 'pointing the finger', the only way to avoid a permanent loss of face was to display a capacity for innovation and to try again to apply the law of action in customer activities, a principle that proved itself when the noiseless switch was made from Alliance I to Alliance II.

The agreement, which was signed after the switch in its original version, probably not least to appease the European approval bodies, contains four other 'back doors':

- violation of the principle of an exclusive dual alliance in theory and in practice
- the non-materialization of the joint holding company to manage joint foreign participations, possibly due to a lack of agreement on its third-country location

- the closure of JVs due to failure to achieve profitability after three years
- the existence, required under the agreement, of a globally applicable valuation standard for a subsequent adjustment of the partners' participations in certain countries.

Of these four hypothetical reasons, probably only the first could potentially have jeopardized the continuation of the alliance.

Overcoming resistance at the partner banks' headquarters

So far, this chapter has looked at different methods of perception and how they are intensified by group-dynamic mechanisms. They are certainly not easily integrated within the scope of a strategic alliance, and it is especially difficult to get the members of middle management at the banks' headquarters, with their special power structures and their own institution-specific interests, to warm to the alliance.

In practice, the key issue centres around whether the social-psychological conditions are more or less the same when a new JV is set up with a specially prepared team as with a 'going concern' that has developed through time to become what it is today. The latter must accept having what, for it, is a completely remote concept of a cross-border cooperation with a foreign partner forced upon it.

What staff at headquarters ask themselves is: does cooperation fit into the programme of a supraregional universal bank? In other words, is not the strategic alliance with a foreign partner bound to remain constantly out-of-step with one's own corporate culture? When one takes a close look at such a head office, it soon becomes apparent that each important division lives a life of its own, which in turn raises some doubts about the notion of a uniform 'corporate culture', since these parts behave largely autonomously towards each other and towards the company as a whole. For this reason one might say they are in a constant cooperation process with each other. Each division – similar to a parliamentary party within a coalition – is forever in search of support for its own particular 'aims' and is prepared to fight for them, if necessary by changing coalitions.

Veiled Franco–German disagreement over corporate governance

The German system of corporate governance, comparable with federalism in politics, centres around the responsibility of the *Fachvorständ* (board member responsible for one or more divisions). Under this system, each member of the board of managing directors ranks equally in every respect with his/her colleagues. This means in effect that he/she cannot be outvoted, since all decisions have to be resolved by the board of managing directors as a whole. Decisions are either passed unanimously or are blocked. However, a compromise may be achieved in that possibilities of 'balancing out' the interests of the individual *Fachvorstände* are discussed and agreed on. When this 'game' works, resignations by *Fachvorstände* out of frustration are relatively rare. The reality is that a *Fachvorständ* must constantly threaten to veto proposals by colleagues who are not wholly supportive of, or who wholly reject proposals concerning, his/her particular division to force them to withdraw their potential veto.[2]

Under the French model, the *Président-Directeur Général* (PDG) is the sole head of the bank. In principle, his responsibility is indivisible, but he can delegate responsibility via a pyramid structure. The members of the top decision-making body also bear special responsibility for the concerns of certain divisions, but they are individually dependent on approval by the PDG. Thus, they have no possibility of vetoing proposals by their colleagues. This model virtually forces them to hand in their resignation when they no longer enjoy the PDG's confidence. The title 'directeur général' states clearly, therefore, where the – indivisible – responsibility for the bank as a whole rests.

This begs the question as to how these two conflicting, national corporate governance styles were actually squared with the requirements of specific 50/50 joint venture units under the BNP/Dresdner alliance. This conflict was not to be resolved by using a smoke-screen of English-language titles; the differences between the modes of thinking at the two banks ran too deep for that.

Eventually, the following way out was adapted: BNP *de facto* used the theory of the prerogative of the *banque de support*, under which the bank in charge of planning and organizing a new JV subsidiary considers the corporate governance of its bank solely to prevail, and tacitly applied the 'agreement of management' that it had drafted. Dresdner Bank, for its part, denied to delegates from its own ranks that it had ever recognized the *banque de support* principle and referred to the 'agreement of management' under which, with regard to the French titles,[3] the corporate governance was to be changed by rotation every five years. Yet no such change ever took place, if only because hardly any colleague remained in position for more than five years, and the respective successors basically had enough on their plates acquainting themselves with their new duties. Thus, there was no need to make a change by rotation at a later point in time. Had a German raised this fundamental question later on, he ultimately would not have received Dresdner's backing.

Generally speaking, it should be relatively easy to eliminate such differences by sensitivity and tact. The French 'co-heads' who know how to 'work' the German system can certainly consider themselves the 'winners', as the German model gives them more strategic room for manoeuvre. By contrast, the French system can produce 'losers' when 'co-head' types with the same qualifications and well-founded concepts encounter one another in a young company. There is no way past the French colleague bearing the more priv- ileged title of 'directeur général' under the *banque de support* system, who discriminates against his German colleague in the latter's specialist field at every turn. This leaves the German with practically no choice other than to hand in her notice and seek a suitable position elsewhere. From the German point of view, on the other hand, to break up such a stalemate situation would be considered the most normal thing in the world.

In reply to the above, however, it may be said that different positions can be just as vehemently defended in the start-up phase of a young joint venture at national level, without cultural differences being responsible. Thus, it is simply a matter of not allowing cultural differences to develop into additional irritating factors. Only the art of de-dramatization, which knows no national boundaries, can ultimately accomplish this.

Four-language approach as the basis of communication in third countries

Let us now turn to the issue of communication, internally and externally, at the JVs of the alliance. The JVs in the reforming states of central and eastern Europe had been established to support the reforming states in modelling their economies along western, market-economy lines. This process involved adapting the structures of economy, government and society to the conditions of world trade, and to open themselves and make themselves transparent for the western banking industry. The western banks engaged in global trade gladly offered their assistance, and met them more than half-way in the geographical sense by establishing a presence at their business centres. It was not considered appropriate to maintain relations with the traditional economies of this region through representative offices alone.

Given the joint ownership of the JVs, the partner banks were obliged to apply for licences for subsidiary banks with a joint capital structure (50/50 JVs). The joint subsidiaries were established as follows: One operative banking unit was responsible for one country, run by an integrated team of French and German nationals. The first and second management levels were composed of expatriates from the partner banks on the principle of parity. Further, an effort was made to recruit, wherever possible, local staff with a command of English, French or German, and to provide them with training in western-style banking before they assumed their posts. Their duties were, above all, to deal with local authorities and customers in the respective local language.

Since the local employees could not act for the JV on their own responsi- bility but only jointly with their superiors, one language was needed as the uniform basis of communication. The creators of the alliance found what seemed to be a clever way out of this dilemma: English, accepted worldwide as the *lingua franca*, was decreed to be the 'language of the partnership'.

This meant that the staff of a Franco–German institution who had agreed to cooperate out of an affiliation to a Franco–German business symbiosis were forced to speak English during business hours, every day. Since scarcely anyone wanted to create a bad impression by violating this official regulation, the JV teams meekly acquiesced and communicated with each other in English.

A second 'command language' may be unavoidable in military affairs where orders are issued and received; but to use a second language in a medium such as banking, which has an extensive and highly differentiated range of specialist terms and definitions and is in close contact with all business sectors as well as legal and economic disciplines, as a vehicle for explaining and understanding complex issues must be seen as a luxury. And if one considers the sheer variety English usage offers, as well as the third countries' own creations of English-language specialist terminology, one will begin to grasp the extra work that went into developing a special English usage in each of the CEE countries.

To this must be added the key reason for establishing business in the individual reforming states, namely to help German and French companies in their search for suitable local business plants. A job of this kind cannot be done without detailed knowledge of German and French business terminology. What had to be processed was a flow of banking-specific information that reached the JVs from the partner banks' home countries each day. It was then evaluated before being passed on in the fourth language within the JV.

Finally, there were the customers of the host country, for whose sake, too, the whole business was carried out.[4] Often they had not yet had an opportunity to learn 'business English' to such an extent that they could use it for negotiation purposes.

This complex language situation made many excessive demands on staff and customers in the third-country business operations of the alliance, purely out of the ambition to make the alliance perfect. During the pioneering days at the start of the 1990s, this extra work may well have been worthwhile in exceptional cases; but, as a permanent condition, with employees receiving competitive remunerations, it simply meant a cost factor of monstrous dimensions.

In other words, the luxury of working with a total of four languages – and of having to pay suitably competitive salaries for the privilege – is a heavy cost burden to bear, and everybody knows how scarce polyglot employees are at a local level.

Notes

1. R. Sennett, *The Corrosion of Character* (New York: W. W. Norton, 1998).
2. This also explains the constant demand by the German partner for 'equality of rights in every respect' for, according to the premises of German corporate governance,

corporate (co-) responsibility, which also covers liability under the German Stock Corporation Act (AktG) of the individual members of the Management Board, is in theory scarcely conceivable without exemption from directives from a higher authority. Where the cooperation is concerned, it is nothing but a stereotyped appeal that the conditions for acting under one's own responsibility remain intact.

3. All members of the top executive body are, with the exception of the PDG, entitled only to the title 'Directeur Général Adjoint'.

4. Cultural awareness training contributed to a better mutual comprehension and to a better functioning of the French–German relationship, it being on the higher level or within the local teams. But these improvements were not sufficient, because they had only a partial impact on the internal situation of the JVs, the culture of the host countries being hereby practically not affected. Therefore, this parameter, for a long time underestimated, had finally to be tackled. (J. Bachèlerie, *Les Cahiers*, No. 9 [September 1998], p. 51.)

10
Business in Central and Eastern Europe in 2000: Dead End for the Alliance?

Complementary interests in corporate banking as the mainstay of the alliance

As has been mentioned several times, strategic consensus for the cooperation between BNP and Dresdner centred around a shared pool of mutual corporate customers whose business opportunities were to be expanded with the help of closely cooperating foreign subsidiaries, loan extensions and other attractive features of the two banks' product ranges. Anything that served this purpose was considered suitable for cooperation, and thoughts of guarding one's own customers were to be thrown overboard.

Sadly, this big-hearted principle proved difficult to implement as it presupposes that the partners are clear about what they want and what they are aiming at; however, it is virtually impossible to prevent personal tactical idiosyncrasies at local level, with the result that any initiatives quickly become disagreeable.

Priority given by both parties to investment banking objectives since 2000

The trend, started by Dresdner Bank when it assumed the leading role in investment banking activities by acquiring Kleinwort Benson, was continued by BNP four years later when it bought Paribas, upgrading investment banking further within the strategic alliance. This was no coincidence, but rather it anticipated a general trend in the market. The global networking of the stock exchanges made it necessary almost everywhere to step up investment banking activities, forcing commercial banking further and further into the background.

Without a doubt there was a worldwide push to improve the supply of companies with equity, whereas more stringent regulatory requirements in the form of equity ratios made it harder for the banks to do so. Moreover, towards the end of the 1990s, there was a year-long stock market boom, putting the buzzword 'emerging markets' on everyone's lips. Competition was becoming increasingly geared towards identifying suitable debtors in the reforming countries of CEE for issues on the global capital markets.

What is more, the investment banking arms of the two partner banks had never been formally included in the cooperation: That is to say, they had never been forced to subject themselves to the code of conduct governing commercial banking. This made the investment bankers something of a joker in the pack. Thus, had a corporate customer mandated a JV of the alliance for a capital market transaction, neither side would have liked to see the lead-manager position allocated to Paribas on the one hand or Kleinwort Benson on the other, by order of the heads of the alliance.

Given that both banks had beefed up their investment banking capacities and that they both subscribed to the strict doctrine of giving investment banking objectives priority when it came to lending, the fiction of fundamentally complementary interests could no longer be sustained. Instead, the partners were forced to concede that the reality in this key sector was characterized by a deep-seated rivalry. For this reason, it was agreed in June 2000 that a solution should be quickly found that allowed each partner to go its own way in investment banking operations in central and eastern Europe.

New constellation in central and eastern European commercial banking

From the year 2000, the earnings situation of the east European joint ventures, the central focus of Alliance II, with their equally balanced organizational charts and their hypertrophic communication set-up with four languages, came under severe pressure. All of a sudden, Dresdner and BNP found themselves confronted, in their own special sector (business with French and German business clients), by apparently better equipped competitors. Market surveys revealed they had been overtaken, on both the German and the French 'flank', by the Bavarian-Austrian HVB/Austria-Creditanstalt on the one hand and Société Générale on the other.[1]

A considerable number of other European large banks, having adopted a different strategy, had taken sizeable shares in the equity of important local CEE banks. Their share in the banking industry in eight CEE countries (aggregate total assets €290.4 billion) climbed from 43 per cent in 2000 to 53 per cent in 2001. This trend underscores a change in the banking landscape of CEE countries, which for the most part had become stabilized in the meantime. Not only did the JVs lose large market shares, but their scope for expansion was also severely reduced as a result. Towards the end of 2000, it became clear that immediate steps had to be taken to change the partners' strategy to enable them to stand their ground in a changed market situation. First, an overnight decision was made to liquidate by March 2001 the joint holding company that had been run in Vienna for just short of two years. As a parallel measure, ownership of each of the JVs in the CEE region was to be passed to one or other of the two partners.

The *banque de support* principle practically begged for this wise decision. Each bank was given back the units for which it had originally been responsible for establishment and organization. Immediately thereafter, the outgoing bank at each JV announced in most cases that it would lose no time in setting up a presence of its own at the respective location, be it in the form of a wholly-owned subsidiary bank or as a branch without its own legal personality, and applications for the necessary permits were filed.

Switch to the customary bi-national, bilingual approach

From then on, the language of the local banking industry became the main language for internal and external communication. Alongside it, the language of the foreign sole shareholder was used to make communication with head office and its corporate customer base as smooth as possible. Although English was still resorted to on certain occasions as a useful means of communicating within the context of the international banking community, it no longer served as the sole binding 'language of command'. It was no longer necessary to celebrate English-language communication all day long. This simplified matters greatly and eased workplace tensions. From a purely organizational point of view it also meant a flattening of hierarchical structures, as well as a marked reduction in the number of expatriates and a massive drive to recruit local staffers. This benefited a new generation of local specialist staff, which in turn fostered a broadening of contacts with local corporate customers.

One example of this new situation is Hungary, where at the initiative of BNP the alliance set up its first JV in 1991. This bank, which developed into a well-known representative of the Hungarian banking sector, became the sole property of BNP in March 2001.

Six months later, Dresdner Bank was awarded a licence and opened in record time its own Dresdner Bank (Hungaria) RT. The workforce planned for this bank was 50 Hungarian colleagues led by the only German national, a general manager with considerable experience in foreign banking. This is probably all that need be said to describe the organizational and communicative structure on which this model, with its sizeable starting workforce, is based. It underlines the fact that German companies are by far the most important foreign group of investors and trading partners in Hungary. Not only large companies but also many small and medium-sized firms are active there. This requires the bank to operate its own banking hall in the Hungarian capital. Of course, in this particular case one ought to bear in mind that the German language is by tradition frequently spoken in Hungary, as it was commonly used in certain circles prior to the two world wars.

The above demonstrates that the conversion of the partner banks' CEE business to a bi-national form of communication with less bureaucracy proved extremely beneficial to both the banks and also to the customers, and might even be considered long overdue. It shows that in an economy as creative as Hungary's, the local business sector needs a larger number of foreign banks, in particular the two pioneering banks, BNP and Dresdner, which, at the very start of the post-Cold War era, accorded this country their respects in 1991.

The alliance partners' involuntary parting of the ways

Why was it that the absolutely normal correction of the partner banks' strategy in CEE business had such a dramatic impact on the alliance itself? Any company that does not want to be left behind by general market developments has no choice but to follow the trend by investing in progress in a timely fashion. Why did this not hold true for the banking partners in this case? It was quite normal to expect that the similarly structured banking markets would one day follow pretty much the same developmental steps to form a new platform. This being so, the question to be asked was simply whether the institutions in place under Alliance II were still up to the task, or was it time for another reform?

The unfortunate thing about this situation was probably the inappropriate procedures used. The partners should have taken steps to ensure that the alliance as an ideational institution did not suffer a loss of prestige. But as a result of this 'salvage campaign', practically its entire portfolio had to be liquidated all at once, taking the ground from under the feet of the alliance.

There was probably not enough time in this precarious situation to conduct detailed talks on the future of the alliance and select new points of focus under Alliance II. The salvage campaign that was carried out in all the countries of CEE left no scope to differentiate. Back in 1995, obviously no one expected that circumstances would one day change abruptly in all the target areas. By closing down the JVs in all CEE countries in one fell swoop, the alliance painted itself into a corner. There was no possibility of avoiding a harrowing loss of face by directing the public's attention to other initiatives of the alliance that had, as a precautionary measure, been developed to a suitably advanced stage. Had this been the case, an automatic hara-kiri effect would not have kicked in.

To put it another way, the decision, based on the merits of the project, to switch from the joint presence in the CEE countries to a separate, simplified presence had become inescapable, and could not be postponed. Just as inescapable were the precautions that had been taken within the scope of the alliance to ensure the continued existence of the partnership as such. How were both measures to be conciliated without damaging one of them? To explain the need for this decision to the public, the augurs and their chief economists should have resorted to the old saying: 'The art of war is adaptable to the situation in hand.'[2]

The situation was undoubtedly most precarious for the local players. Because of the task thrust upon them they must have felt – without any reorientation envisaged for the alliance – as if they were digging the alliance's grave. To put it another way, they found themselves in much the same position as someone who, after a hefty debate, decides to leave the room because of the mess and take to another which he assumes exists next-door, but the door thought to lead to the room next-door proves to be the outside door. Much to his surprise, the person vacating the room finds himself in the inhospitable outdoors. The illusion of a house shared has been shattered. As there was no longer any prescribed joint path for them to take, each party had to head disconsolately and alone for home.

Since, in the previous three years, both partners had seen fundamental changes to the structure of their share capital which radically altered the self-image and the strategic position of both banks, each tried to shrug off the shift in the alliance, pointing to its own new position and strategic orientation. Having taken over Paribas in 1998, BNP felt stronger and better equipped as a result, and philosophized about its having long since outgrown the alliance in any case. The same feeling prevailed at Dresdner which, following its merger with Allianz Versicherungen in 2001, suddenly found itself with the equity base it needed to realize the banking strategy it had dreamed of under the *bancassurance* strategy (combining banking with assurance and insurance products) as a member of the Allianz Group.

Reasons for organizational shortcomings in cross-border banking activities

A big bank that forms an alliance with a big bank abroad to engage in joint operations in third countries needs considerable surpluses of tangible and human resources, since it not only has to shoulder extraordinary investment costs but must also have funds for product development at the ready. These investments, lest one forget, have to be financed in addition to the wide-ranging improvements in the local competitive situation which are indispensable for a constant 'all-round renewal' of the domestic network.

Thus, when a bank already has to bear the heavy financial burden of an extraordinary local project such as Dresdner in the years 1990–4, when all at once it had to establish new domestic branches in what was once its central German homeland, it is forced to accept that it no longer has sufficient funds at its disposal for its foreign network and foreign product lines. But if a bank nevertheless decides to abide – for the most part, on a verbal basis – by the strategic concept of the alliance involving spectacular foreign undertakings, the suspicion that this is a sham manoeuvre cannot be readily dismissed.[3]

This illustrates that a partner who is prepared to make the necessary material, personnel and financial resources available for a strategic alliance abroad will have a tremendous price to pay, for the survival of the shared myth calls for all manner of sacrifices as an absolutely vital prerequisite for later expansions at a transnational level: sacrifices that only truly cosmopolitan strategists are capable of making. On the other hand, a partner who believes he can dispense with far-sighted measures to safeguard the joint business policy and achieve his objective by more economical means fails to appreciate the safeguarding framework needed in terms of capital and organization to keep the shared myth from suddenly crashing to earth. The potential that either partner in an alliance might overestimate their own capabilities at any time basically feeds a source of endless uncertainty. This shows how thin the ice is when it comes to handling the organizational problems to be mastered.

When two perceptions (resulting from different perspectives) clash, the question that inevitably arises is whether a uniform perception of circumstances beyond the 'domestic/foreign' borderline is actually possible from two local standpoints. The following occurrences from day-to-day dialogue between BNP and Dresdner make this point clear.

1 When, for example, representatives from international and domestic business within one and the same bank discuss the purpose of a strategic alliance at a transnational level, a consensus is usually not reached. The differences in the objectives each has in mind are normally too great.
2 At meetings of the international bankers of both banks or of the domestic branches of both banks, conflicts arise because one side is unable to comprehend oddities in the other's line of reasoning. Each side approaches the issue in hand differently, sets different priorities, and so on, and the partners are beset by intercultural differences as a result of internalized perspectives which, it transpires, do not match.
3 Virtual helplessness prevails when an international banker from one side has to grasp statements by a domestic banker from the other. In such a case, pretty well all the parameters described above become tangled up, making it difficult to tell 'the bottom' from 'the top'.

How, one cannot help but ask, is the formation of a joint will possible on a basis such as this? Is there any chance that the parties concerned can succeed in achieving a shared vision of their undertaking? The ability of shared geographical and statistical aids to remedy this ill is limited because joint positions, in turn, call for interpretation; and, once again, both partners view the question from the vantage point of their own individual perspective.

The dangerous thing when attempting to form a joint will appears to be that a forming strength lies within every perspective, as a result of which the party concerned is directed (as if on rails) as to how he perceives. To the onlooker, that party seems to be a prisoner of his own perspective.

In truth, every standpoint is constituted by itself in that every subject perceives and assesses the world from within their own national system of coordinates. Everything – occurrences, principles, and so on – that takes place or exists congruently to that system quite naturally constitutes the subject's inner world. As its direct opposite, the subject experiences everything that cannot be placed within his or her system of coordinates as 'the' outside world, that which is 'foreign' or 'alien', which in itself is very strangely structured.

What insights are to be gained from this analysis? The question to be asked is this: is it possible to find some kind of solution to the constant divergences between local and international perspectives to the extent that a minimum of 'action' is necessary? Or does it call for a different kind of guideline to take the place of an illusory consensus on the interpretation of deductive principles? The most likely alternative are authorities in agreement in the guise of charismatic leader-types, referred to in the above connection as 'augurs'.

Integral tendencies of cultural perspectives with the risk of a crumbling consensus

An alliance entered into for an indefinite period calls for a convergence of its systems of references as the cornerstone of a longest-possible continuance of a basic consensus in an undertaking such as this. This does not rule out the possibility that one day, quite unintentionally, changes might occur in both parties' systems of references, as a result of which certain shifts in the underlying assumptions can no longer be ignored. In order to put things to rights, not only a target-oriented, forward-looking joint venture, but also an appropriate procedure for reaching a modified consensus are called for.

However, because neither side finds this an easy thing to do, the process of overhauling outdated shared objectives turns out to be extremely difficult. This is intensified as the partners concern themselves with the details, for by doing so they enter the hazy terrain of cultural self-images, to tolerate which demands almost more greatness from one's partner since, as a result of psychological inevitabilities, each partner tends at first to look upon the other's departure from the given consensus as a deficit of reliability. In fact, what both partners are seeking to do is, first, to establish their own and (for them) an absolutely normal system of references and, for another, to preserve the consistency of the system of what has been agreed on to date – the supposed essence of the alliance – to prevent the fundamental consensus from falling apart.

This makes clear why local and international perspectives and interests cannot, as a rule, be reduced to a common denominator, for that would mean that each inner-world perspective, an expression of each partner's independence, conforms on a permanent basis with that of a competing counterpart. In a sense, this is good news for the antitrust watchdogs everywhere. They do not need to put so much thought into rules and regulations. In the long run, the 'fission fungus' that finds its way into crevices between the different perspectives does the job for them. Of course, concepts pertaining to the joint undertaking abroad, in third countries, suffer most because the ground both partners have in common is supposed to be reflected in the shaping of special banking services. The truth is that a harmony of this kind is by nature more of a coincidence.

One example is shown by the converging, organizational fundamental structures at both banks at the beginning of the agreement. At the start of the 1990s, the organizational structures of both head offices were based on a strict division between domestic business and international business. This could be seen as a promising starting-point for possible convergences, synergies and effects of scale.

Dresdner *de facto* put an end to this initial homogeneity in the mid-1990s, following the 'Walter reform' of corporate customer banking at Dresdner's head office when the two mutually exclusive perspectives, domestic and international, were merged for rationalization reasons. Henceforth there was no chance of identifying structural counterparts as the cooperation agreement had required. Dresdner had decided to rid itself of this rigid differentiation because it forced the bank to deploy a double troop of product specialists. The signal that went out was that from now on, only product specialists attending primarily to local operations and, in addition, capable of occasionally working with foreign customers as well, would be tolerated.[4]

BNP, on the other hand, stuck to the course it had mapped out for itself in that it divided its entire organization in two and rebuilt the two separate entities from the bottom up. In taking these measures, BNP signalled the future viability of its foreign business just as it did its local branch network. Thus, the territorial principle became the dividing line within the bank's organization.

As early as the second half of the 1990s, this disharmony gave warning of a decline in convergence between the foreign policy of each partner bank due to a steady growing apart of the partners' perspectives with regard to foreign business. Strict adherence to the territorial principle has long been one fundamental difference between the perspectivistic orientation of the government sector and the business sector in Germany. For decades, government bodies have been able to focus their planning activities purely on the national perspective. They are able quite simply to ignore matters such as cross-border transport in their transport planning. In this way, railway networks have their own natural boundaries within which transport planning is confined. Through the German constitution, responsibilities are assigned solely according to the following categorization: local matters are dealt with by the Länder (federal states), while issuers concerning the state as a whole *vis-à-vis* other countries are the responsibility of the Bund (German federal government), an arrangement that makes as much sense today as on the day it came into effect.

In business, on the other hand, a direct link has always existed between domestic sales and foreign selling markets. This is why research and development – to say nothing of specific product development and market launches – have to be closely aligned to foreign systems of norms.

The banks, for their part, since they are tied primarily to their national currency, operate chiefly (like the government bodies) on the territorial principle. However, banks are relatively autonomous in how, technically, they conduct their foreign business. The lines of contact to the local branch exist purely in terms of capital and personnel. Strategically, foreign business takes its cue indirectly from domestic business via the local corporate clients, for whose sake – so the banks constantly assure them – they brave the inclemency of the foreign markets. Thus, the needs of customers in third countries and the relevance of own-account deals to the interbank sector count for little by comparison.

On the other hand, a mixture of local and international perspectives which, by their very nature, isolate and exclude each other, predominate in the field of action of cross-border activities, such as the bodies of the European Union, the European Parliament, the EU Commission and the EU Court of Justice. The special handicap in the case of the Parliament is that it does not have the awareness of a European public on its side at a social and political level to define issues of interest, and which is supported and monitored by its own pluralistically structured party and press system.

Similarly, BNP and Dresdner had taken it upon themselves to create a hybrid union of complementary perspectives as the objective of their strategic alliance. That is why this objective was made the subject of the preamble to the agreement. Certainly, this happened without the slightest misgiving, the partners assuming that reference to the exalted political order of the European Communities would remove, virtually on its own, any doubts harboured by the private enterprise sector. The partner banks thought they could dispense with the underlying radical, anthropological question as to whether anyone had ever provided evidence that such a 'blend' of local and – at least in part – mutually exclusive perspectives is conceivable and that it lends itself to systematic organization.

Must one assume, then, that the joint undertaking of BNP and Dresdner was ultimately felled by a *petitio principi* (assuming a principle)? In other words, did an unproven precondition serve (impermissibly in terms of logic) as the argument for the correctness of a statement? The claim made was that the cooperative concept of BNP and Dresdner was in a position to reconcile disparate, conflicting banking business perspectives. The way in which the two banks parted company during the central and eastern European crisis shows this supposition to be neither founded nor unfounded. If there were some indications in the positive sense, this would mean that it is in principle possible for groups of people to free themselves from their own national system of references to such an extent that they could, as a strategic alliance, conceive a Euroland business policy in its own right and carry it through. This would be evidence that there could be such a thing as a pan-European business policy capable of existing independently of big domestic-market perspectives.

What would be the consequence if such were not the case? One would simply have to assume that the transnational strategic alliance was bound to fail. It was doomed to failure from the beginning because competitive pressure on the large local banking markets remained so intense as to make the market participants totally indifferent to the opportunities on neighbouring banking markets. On the other hand, there was little chance of a large overlapping market emerging.

We owe the assumption in the last sentence to the partner banks themselves. In March 2001, they announced that BNP Paribas had acquired, in the consumer credit market, a 70 per cent stake in WKV Bank from Dresdner Bank. This meant a return to the classical practice of acquiring company stakes, as if the cooperation agreement had never existed.

The ongoing presence of the shared myth of BNP and Dresdner Bank

The public end of the cooperation agreement between BNP and Dresdner came with a joint Press Release on 4 October 2002:

> BNP Paribas and Dresdner Bank have reached an amicable understanding to terminate the cooperation agreement between the two institutions in the fields of banking and bank-related business, which has been in place since 1996.
>
> In a recently signed rescission agreement, both partners concluded that the objectives of the cooperation agreement were no longer valid in view of subsequent changes in market conditions and in view of the divergences in strategic development of the two institutions. It was therefore agreed that the accord should be formally terminated.
>
> The possibilities of future cooperation in specific business areas, built on the special relationship of trust built up over the past years, will be explored. One example of this is the joint venture Cetelem Bank GmbH.

Mr Michel Pébereau will step down from the Dresdner Bank Supervisory Board at elections scheduled for the coming year. At the same time, Dr Bernd Farholz will resign his position as a member of the Board of Directors of BNP Paribas.

What remains? When one asks, in retrospect, what insights the ten-year experiment of the strategic alliance between BNP and Dresdner produced, the role of a shared myth warrants special attention. The way in which this myth – to the surprise of many – soared like a comet and created, thanks to its suggestive strength, a field of sympathy and expectation, was extraordinary. Unfortunately, it cannot be said to have achieved anything. This may be explained above all by the fact that the enticing PR announcements hurried on ahead of the actual possibilities of product development. Neither did the partners have at their disposal an adequate financial cushion to cover the extraordinary investments to be made in their joint business activities, and for these reasons the tremendous potential of well-disposed public interest that had been kindled went unused.

Given the time and work that have to be invested in creating artificial myths, and in light of the scant prospects of actually doing so, the lack of consideration for the needs of an already-existing, viable, natural myth appears doubly lamentable.

Chapters 4 and 6 have already described the tremendous implications of the shared myth for the alliance in the eyes of the public. Like a living being with changing ideas and suggestions, it forms the dynamic core of the alliance as the 'third member' of the team. It personifies – albeit unconsciously – a cross-section of the expectations of the public from the perspective of consumers, the media, competitors and the capital markets. One could describe it as a (highly sensitive) 'co-entrepreneur' who constantly wants to be fed and entertained with announcements and events, for it is aware of the power it possesses to initiate, to accelerate or to stop developments through its suggestive strength.

It was, therefore, a severe loss when the partner banks, caught off guard by the adverse turn of events on the banking markets in CEE, failed to properly assess the exceptional value of their shared myth as the heart of future joint undertakings within the scope of the alliance, and to save it from crashing earthwards by unhitching it from CEE policy in good time. Instead, the partners were forced, having misread the situation, to drop the strategic alliance like a hot potato.

Realistically, the shared myth could easily have continued to give the partners important impetus and support as a special strategic aid (provided, however, its benefactors had been prepared to see and recognize this factor as such). Herein lay the problem of the two big banks which, out of pride at what they had achieved locally, failed to retract their domestic, national myths to such an extent that they would not inflict lasting damage on their rival, the transnational, pan-European myth of the alliance.

In consideration of the above, one must emphasize that only a shared myth conceived for the long term is in a position to give rise to and support transnational contacts in that concepts for organizational forms and business strategies are set up on this foundation, piece by piece.

A discarded myth only seemingly sinks into oblivion; it continues to exist at a virtual level as a precedent, and as such can cause unpleasant after-effects. For example, it could be capable of mobilizing scepticism as regards the repetition of such an exercise, much as an unsuccessful previous marriage might. Prejudices of this kind are likely to live a long and vigorous life, and to go on producing negative feedback.

International strategic alliances can, in principle, contribute towards the Europeanization of banking, though within limits. If this ongoing paradigm change leads to the structural break-up of the type of bank that has predominated thus far, the idea of complementary links in the form of a strategic alliance may well be revived, provided the customers see there is something in it for them.

Notes

1. *Süddeutsche Zeitung*, 10 September 2001.
2. The alliance partners could have indicated that it might make sense, within a certain period of time (for example, until the euro had been introduced in the countries of central and eastern Europe), to group the separate units together again given that a great deal more could be achieved in the region as a whole with an expanded equity base. Prospects of this kind can have a 'sound' foundation. After all, all the parties concerned – including the stock exchanges – are interested in shaping, with time, more and more reliable perspectives for the future.
3. This conflict was, in essence, typical of the fortunes of Dresdner Bank from 1996 onwards, when it took on a further financial burden in the form of global primary market operations by acquiring Kleinwort Benson. The available capital base proved to be too weak to support the many different business policies. This finally led to the desperate attempt to offer itself in a 'merger of equals' with Deutsche Bank. When this failed, Dresdner tried in vain to strengthen its financial position by taking over Commerzbank. Not until Dresdner was taken over by Allianz AG on the basis of an integrated financial services provider concept did the former receive the boost it needed to actually fill the broad-based business structures, although even that was not possible without self-imposed restrictions in Dresdner's foreign activities (such as abandonment of mainstream activities in the USA and Japan). The moral is, he who tries to do everything at once is bound to take a fall eventually.
4. This was an unmistakable indication that Dresdner considered the opportunities in foreign business to be limited in the longer term, and that at some point the bank would withdraw from globally oriented foreign activities. Dresdner was clever enough quickly to include the EU member states in the local business

category, allowing the bank to present itself overnight as the 'European adviser bank'. To believe that, in so doing, Dresdner had cancelled out at a stroke the subtle antagonisms between the local perspectives of the (at national level) highly differing EU member states is tantamount to a strategic folly; or was it only an impulsive, premature forward move on the strategic battlefield? Time will tell.

Part II

The Structural Crisis of Traditional Banking

11
Universal Banking: From National Peculiarity to Ideology

Defining 'ideology'

'Ideology' as a sociological term needs first to be clarified, for it is a phenomenon related to the 'myth'. But whereas the myth is of an ephemeral nature in that it automatically becomes superfluous as soon as its tangibly perceptive 'peg' disappears, ideology is able to stand on its own virtually for all time as a strictly rational, systematically developable statement within the communicative context of the world of ideas, and so enter into an autonomous relationship with the topical issues of an epoch by installing itself elsewhere, true to the principle of the boundless freedom of thought.

According to the sociological view adopted here,[1] ideologies are essentially inadequately communicated intellectual realities with a disturbed or falsified foundation in the sensorily verifiable reality. These para-theoretical statements on certain subjects may be qualified as an ideology if characterized by a rigidly argumentative typification. Such intelligible statements may be passed on and infiltrated in an uncontrollable manner as benchmarks and as role models.

However, it is also conceivable that an idea could come into being based on a certain generally valid principle which originally had a sound reference to a certain section of verifiable reality, but subsequently the value of its statement, due to excessive generalization, could appear highly dubious due to historical shifts on the reality level. It then mutates into ideology in that it becomes too far removed from its factual basis. It takes on a life of its own having become a faded, unspecific, hackneyed principle, and is passed from one person to the next as 'gospel'. What is so critical about this phenomenon is that because it possesses a considerable degree of pseudo-scientific plausibility it prevents deeper, contemporary ideas of real challenges from materializing.

Extensive self-regulation of German banking at the dawn of industrialization

The banking model of Imperial Germany since the start of the nineteenth century has been characterized by great restraint on the part of legislators in regulating the banking sector and the way in which the capital market operates. The universal banking system, which emerged as the fruit of economic liberalism around the mid-nineteenth century (before the unification of Germany in 1871), leaves it to the forces of the crystallizing economic society to develop their own banking system and, to this end, to look for suitable role models abroad. The high degree of acceptance this system was quickly afforded soon gave it the status of a national accomplishment. Their economic role acknowledged, the banks were able systematically to set about developing appropriate strategic objectives.

Manfred Pohl,[2] a historian of German banking, identifies six stages in the development of Germany's banking system:

1. 1848–72   Waves of foundations
2. 1895–1924 The systematic formation of the system
3. 1924–33   Stabilization during the global economic and banking crisis
4. 1933–45   Universal banks under the dictatorship of National Socialism
5. 1946–56   Reshaping of the banking system after the Second World War
6. 1957–86   Concentration and restructuring to accommodate retail banking

Dispensing with strategic restrictions under the universal banking system

According to H. E. Büschgen,[3] a 'universal bank' is defined as a credit institution which subjects itself to absolutely no selection criteria, whether in terms of quantity, region, location, human resources, business sector or quality.

A principle of this kind which is open in all directions and dispenses with all the usual dimensions and criteria postulates absolute flexibility, pure pragmatism, as the highest business policy value. Everything hinges, as the macro-economic situation permits, on whether one operates offensively or defensively. This shows that the accoutrements of the joint stock company had changed nothing of the traditional pragmatism of the eighteenth- or nineteenth-century private banker who weighed up the specific opportunities and risks of each and every day and mapped out his business strategy accordingly.

Thus it was many years until the era of the so-called product specialists at the beginning of the twentieth century, who sought to standardize the more common banking services with a view to marketing them systematically within a clearly contoured competitive environment. The main characteristic of the beginning of the universal banking era was the co-existence of lending and securities business and, building upon that, the industrial holding company. Essentially, the universal banks' secret lay in the ability to 'juggle these balls' at the same time, and it was with this ability that the private bankers of the eighteenth and nineteenth centuries had grown up; furthermore, they brought this ability with them into the newly founded joint stock banks, where they continued to hold key positions in the supervisory boards for decades.

It was not until after 1895 that private banker status lost more and more significance in the banking sector. One main reason for this was that such bankers' equity, as well as their deposits and borrowed funds, were insufficient to prefinance issues for the evolving large companies or to grant them adequate loans for investment purposes.

What institutions acted as the role-models of their age? The first universal bank in banking history was Société des Pays-Bas, established in the Netherlands in 1822. Moreover, it was the first bank in Europe that also considered business start-ups and trade investments as belonging to its core activities. A further role-model was Crédit-Mobilier, which was founded in Paris in 1852 and attracted a great deal of attention by the way it opened itself to a broad national public.

In Germany, by contrast, which until 1872 was a collection of sovereign principalities, the public was still only regionally structured in the mid-nineteenth century. There was the private banking house, Abraham Schaafhausen, in Cologne, the legal form of which was changed in 1848 to create Schaafhausen'scher Bankverein, the first German joint stock bank.

The main point German legislators expected of the joint stock banks, and one that was difficult to impose on them at legislative or regulatory level, was that they shape an efficient capital market on the basis of the newly created territorial currency and legal uniformity of the German Reich. Significantly, the term *Gründerzeit* (literally, period of founders) was soon commonly used to describe this period because of the rapid expansion and new creations it brought forth.

This charged field gave rise to a network of relationships that was reflected in strategy in the following ways.

1 In the field of stock issues, the German universal banks operated together in syndicates to provide the joint stock companies of the country – not always under convenient circumstances – with special services in procuring and restructuring risk capital. The issuance of new shares was subject, according to the autonomously arranged consortium practices, to a permanently existing banking syndicate with permanent members (each with fixed underwriting shares) and lead management by one or more large banks. In addition, they were involved as members of broad-based issue

syndicates in the issuance of government bonds, industrial bonds and foreign bonds.

2   Thus, industrial clients who maintained a relationship with the universal bank as principal banker and syndicate leader could happily leave their worries about their equity requirements and their needs for external financing to their principal banker, which would take the necessary steps in good time. From 1885 to 1924, the universal banks concentrated primarily on acting as the 'issuing and speculation bank'. Subsequently, the focus was put on deposits and lending.

3   An opportunity for external growth occasionally presented itself in that the share capital of banks which found themselves in financial difficulties was taken over in the interest of the stability of the national economy. In just a few decades, successive takeovers by Berlin's big four banks gave rise to nationwide branch networks. Whereas Dresdner Bank had 36 branch establishments at the end of 1916, the number had risen to 86 by the end of 1926.

4   The 'brains trust' at the central organization focused on three departments: corporate loans, syndication and the stock exchange. The corporate loans department was responsible for coordinating loan decisions. Since the special expertise for assessing the different business sectors was gathered here, this was the preferred recruiting ground for top executives.

5   The stock exchange department saw to stock exchange trading in the sense of secondary market dealings with securities traded nationwide. This department coordinated the bank's presence at the various regional stock exchanges and serviced wealthy private clients with a special interest in securities.

6   The syndication department was, as the 'wholesaler', responsible for primary market operations, the market for new issues. Moreover, it acted as contact partner for permanent contacts among syndicate banks.

Industrial customers and their principal bankers

In the 150-year history of German industrialization, the German corporate customer saw its partnership with a specific universal bank as its central pillar in the economic and monetary ups and downs of the nineteenth and twentieth centuries. The implications of this symbiotic cooperation were many. The principal banker usually served on the supervisory board and was thus able to act as mediator between company and investors. The benefits of a strong 'umbrella' in the financial sector were beyond doubt. Who or what could shake the standing of a big German bank?

It is here that the roots of the oft-quoted 'Deutschland AG' (corporate Germany) and, on the other hand, of a permanent pampering of German companies with their underdeveloped financial awareness lie. Companies apparently preferred to have their principal banker relieve them of the finance-related tasks, allowing them to concentrate on technological progress and their markets. In addition, the fateful tendency to give preference to flexible external financing in the form of cash loans over complex equity financing solutions has its roots in this attitude. It is no mere coincidence that the capital ratio at medium-sized British companies is traditionally twice as high as that of their counterparts of the German *Mittelstand* (middle-range companies).

The age of retail banking as the end of the development

Whereas the banking industry's contribution to the gross national product was only 0.5 per cent at the end of the nineteenth century, it was 1.8 per cent in 1950, a good 2.5 per cent in 1968 and more than 4 per cent in 1991.[4] In other words, Germany's banking sector grew almost ten times as fast as the rest of the economy in the twentieth century; but then came the turning point. A dramatic downturn can be observed since the year 2000 as the growth potential is felt to have been totally exhausted.

There are a number of reasons for this. One of them lies in the fact that corporate headquarters now act like banks in that they themselves tap the capital markets to raise funds for buyers and suppliers. Cash management systems, moreover, have reduced the banks' share in companies' financial operations.

Innovation stakes from the mid-1950s lead to a twin-track banking strategy

The above principle of a systematic 'division of labour' between the commercial banks and corporate customers proved to be a blessing for the German economy, particularly between the two world wars and again in the post-war period. As far as the customers were concerned there was little reason to seek an alternative. Any company with a certain minimum standard of creditworthiness was practically assured that the principal banker and the syndicate it headed would, also in future, see to its finance requirements. The likelihood that a large bank might itself run into difficulties was, according to previous experience, virtually zero.

The question, therefore, was whether the banks could continue to dispense with strategic differentiations in the face of a changing competitive environment. To keep existing customers happy, the banks gave them to understand that they still considered themselves all-round experts in all product fields, and intended to operate as such in future. In a manner of speaking, the banks were willing to grant their customers maximum benefit from banking technical advancements. Further, they assured their customers that they would do everything they could to continue offering them 'prime terms'; but these were not the beginnings of a new strategic solution.

Meanwhile, the rapid industrial expansion of the second half of the 1950s, the 1960s and the early 1970s had created an industrial context that should have put paid to the banks' desire to hold on to their traditional customer base at any price, if only for reasons of risk diversification, as a spread of lending risks according to objective, geographical and business-sector criteria was sorely lacking.

From the point of view of marketing policy, on the other hand, prestige considerations made it seem highly advisable for the banks to emphasize their universal know-how in all product fields. They were loath to point out to existing customers the convincing, objective reasons why they ought to try to find another banking connection. After all, this tactic did not rule out the fact that they could express an interest in acquiring new customers as well. When new companies evolved and the position of principal banker was still to be filled, the banks were willing to go to great lengths to present themselves as a suitable candidate. The consequence was a twin-track strategy, a game played by two sets of rules. And, when in doubt, the good old universal banking strategy would win the day.

What is more, the German banks typically still felt, through the training sector they together supported, an obligation to the dogmatic unity of banking. No one had anything to gain by disturbing this canon of a banking-sector-wide, product-related system. The banks, then, were anxious to go on demonstrating to the public that the banking world was in order.

The only factor that could have brought change within the context of the new competitive situation was the behaviour of the customers themselves. A company that considered itself, thanks to its attractive credit quality, strong enough to test its market value could ultimately dare to try the tactical move of threatening to terminate the relationship with its principal banker to obtain more favourable terms. There was little the bank could do, when blackmailed in this way, if it did not want to contribute towards the demolition of the principle it held sacred. For this reason, the bank had no choice but to compromise, even though the new margin – slimmer than that previously in place – ate at the profitability of the relationship. The important thing was that outwardly the universal banking principle remained intact.

This was and is the downside of the much-praised universal banking system, and is essentially the reason why for decades German banks consistently generated appreciably lower earnings than foreign banking institutions. When caught between customers' interests and shareholders' interests, the banks were always willing to play safe with the customers; the shareholders, despite all the solemn declarations that were made to the contrary, came off second-best.

At the heart of this competitive deadlock were the big banks which, given their market position on the financial markets – and, on the strength of that, their supposed strategic far-sightedness – had enough authority as 'leaders of the herd' to be able to present their own solutions as opinion-formers to the public. These proposals had every chance of being accepted and, with that, of having a pioneering effect. But because the 'herd' followed their lead, the system – and therefore the competitive behaviour – ultimately remained the same. No bank had to go out on a limb, and all were able to offer their customers innovations of the same quality.

Autonomous business field strategies undermine the universal banks' image

After the banks switched, in the 1980s, to establishing new business arms as specialist banks – for example, mortgage banks or institutions offering leasing, factoring and direct banking services – a question arose as to their strategic orientation. Should they, outwardly, be an integral part of the bank as a whole or should they be allowed to operate relatively autonomously? The latter option appeared to be inevitable.

Thus developed the theory of strategic thinking in terms of strategic business fields (SBFs) and strategic business units (SBUs). What was so special about them was that they took their bearings from customer groups instead of, as in the past, product groups. An SBF is more individually oriented towards a more strongly segmented market and towards a distinct customer group. The customer group, in turn, is oriented towards certain elements of the product range offered by the bank as a whole (according to the regionally defined spheres of responsibility) to solve their finance problems.

As an organizational unit of the bank, an SBU assumes the task of running a certain SBF independently. The SBU decides how its financial, personnel and material resources are to be deployed. Its business-field-specific market responsibility, therefore, is to draw up and implement its own operative plans in a market with precisely identifiable customers and competitors, and then to run a check of the results.

A business field strategy determines what objectives will be aimed at and by what means, and what forms of behaviour have to be developed to this end. Certain functions such as marketing, organization, HR and IT absolutely must be performed autonomously. The most important difference compared with earlier practice is that strategies and plans of action no longer need to be established step by step over several hierarchical levels (a procedure during which the special intentions of the strategy in question always become less focused).

During this process, the bank as a whole saw itself with no alternative other than to adapt more and more to pluridisciplinary strategies. Outwardly, subordination to the autonomous profiles of other SBUs was on no account to be conveyed. How otherwise could the bank accentuate its image of being run as one complete entity? But in desiring the superordinated coordination it itself practised in the sense of an overarching, overall profile, was it not getting in its own way? Certainly, it would be preferable if the different SBUs could present to the market a uniform, united image of the bank as such. But is not, of all things, the assured autonomy given to individual SBUs *vis-à-vis* their neighbouring SBUs bound to spawn disunity within such a large company? Just as unavoidable in cases where different SBUs have a competitive interest in what are, in fact, mutual clients are signs of jealousy, ongoing rivalry and creeping alienation.

Since the organs of the bank as a whole are responsible for the distribution of resources, they are, without doubt, able to win a certain respect for themselves in this way. However, the universal bank can no longer be thought capable of wielding the same business-steering influence it once did. The players' real attention is fixed on the rivals in each division. The pressure to succeed weighing on all SBUs means that in-house connections to other SBUs are, as a rule, poorly developed. Cross-selling remains sterile theory. This explains why, for example, joint acquisition trips and other cost synergy-driven measures within the scope of the bank as a whole have little chance of being put into practice.

The bank–customer interface, therefore, shifts from one strategic business field to another according to the action required. Thanks to the flat hierarchy, the main players at the bank, an autonomous team of specialists, are able to conclude their own business transactions themselves without any delay. This they are forced to do not least because the competitive constellation varies widely from business field to business field. Thus, the activities as a whole are determined by different market potentials and lead to different profit calculations. For this reason, the question to be asked is: where, in such a situation, is the superordinated, ordering influence of the bank as a whole? A relatedness of this kind results purely, as in the days of the jack-of-all-trades universal bank, from the length of the hierarchical decision-making channel. Progress has its price.

Now that the parties involved in the bank–customer interface make the relevant decisions in direct contact with each other, it is not surprising that the profile of the bank as a whole is being increasingly forced into the background. It is the different implications of each market segment that give every special type of business its own unmistakable stamp and its own individual dynamism. The organs of the bank as a whole still exert their influence to present to the marketplace the image of a uniform, united bank.

Certainly, as far as the customer is concerned, the quality of the service is no longer determined by the prestige of the parent bank that can 'do it all', but by the tried and tested expertise of the respective autonomously operating teams, which could just as well be disincorporated to form a separate joint stock company.

'At daggers drawn': commercial banking and investment banking

The fundamental understanding that exists between commercial banking and investment banking stems from the difference between their basic strategic approach, which runs like a red thread through the methodology of both camps and makes itself felt whenever it comes to servicing what are virtually identical customer groups. Nevertheless, each camp is dependent on close cooperation with the other, as neither can perform the role the other has to play.

At first glance, the object of their endeavours looks the same in that both camps set about grouping, each in its own way, certain companies according to national and international criteria and market developments as they seek ways of improving these companies' financial resources on a lasting basis. However, this classification is done according to different macro-economic and micro-economic criteria and standards. The consequence of the difference in approach is that it is often impossible to agree on what measures are best suited to the customer's interests.

Investment banking as a medium depends on stock market acceptance, whereas commercial banking hinges solely on customer acceptance. Expertise in the latter case is expressed in a sympathetic understanding of the special nature of the customer's sector and the customer's present situation. In stark contrast to this, the symbolic strength of the product range in investment banking outweighs national and cultural ties to the home market inasmuch as the investment banker has to do the worldwide analysis for investors and issuers of securities in globally networked financial markets.

Cooperation between the two camps may typically be as follows. First and foremost, the investment banker is ruled entirely by what happens on the various financial markets. If he spots, somewhere, signs of a positive trend that might be used to put together an offer of some kind, his (secondary) interest is to cast the leading role, that of debtor of an issue, as well as he can. The list of possible candidates is long. But who knows the top managers at this or that company? Who has their confidence? From this moment on, cooperation with commercial banking comes into play. Contacts have to be arranged, and fast. People have to be persuaded that a unique opportunity has presented itself for their company, and that this opportunity has to be seized without delay. It is not so much a case of whether or not the flaws in such an opportunity have been spotted; once the rest of the cast has been finalized, the important point is to confront the market with the offer at the peak of its upward trend, for this is when the probability is greatest that the customer will 'bite'.

Cooperation within the framework of the old universal bank

In the traditional universal bank the relationship between the commercial banking department and the investment banking department was like that between general practitioner and medical specialist. Since the contact with the customer at local level was the privilege of the regional network and served commercial banking purposes only, investment banking activities were concentrated at head office as a kind of virtual bank. It was up to the organs of the commercial banking department to decide when a certain customer should be taken to the capital market. Only then were the colleagues from head office presented to the customer, who could henceforth reckon with additional service from this corner of the bank. The mediators from commercial banking watched jealously over every step their colleagues took, and were to be informed of everything in advance.

When the specific timetable for the issue was to be compiled, the commercial banking camp again assumed control via its procedural guidelines for approving (credit) risks inasmuch as it had to make the final decision regarding the capital market transaction in the interest of the bank as a whole (shortly before entering the market) according to the formal criteria of a lending transaction.

In short, the relationship was that between 'master' and 'maid', as the relationship between theology and philosophy in the Middle Ages has been described. Although there would by all means be words of praise this did not mean the slightest indication of harmony. On the other hand, the economically closed involvement of the investment bankers made sure that a limited number of specialists were deployed, making costs easily controllable. What is more, the capital market was not overtaxed by excessive activity, which had the effect of stabilizing the price level.

The reversal of the situation at the end of the 1990s

The investment banking arm was the first to benefit from the gradual emancipation, described above, of the segments within the universal bank. Since roughly the start of the 1980s, the London branches of the US investment banks have been so successful with their business methods in primary market trading in stocks and bonds, as well as with their consultancy services in company takeovers, that the rest of the market has been forced to assume these new standards.

When, in 1989 and 1995 respectively, Germany's two leading universal banks, Deutsche Bank and Dresdner Bank, took over Morgan Grenfell and Kleinwort Benson, London's two largest investment banks, their impact on the overall structure at both banks was irresistible until, finally, the prevailing influence of commercial banking over investment banking was virtually reversed.

As the flow of loan extensions to companies grew more and more weak and a new criterion was needed to regulate this flow optimally in the interest of the bank as a whole, the willingness to mandate future capital market transactions became the criterion for the lending bank. With that, the commercial banking arm was more or less relegated to the role of feeder to the investment banking camp.

Whatever the future developments as a direct result of the stock market collapse that has shaken the world since 2001, the losers are – for the first time since 1929 – bank shares and, above all, shares of the typical universal banks. Long pronounced dead, the universal bank is unlikely to escape radical change now. Since the two antagonists have now succeeded in robbing each other of their ability to act, a formal separation is inevitable this time around. Chapter 14 will deal in depth with the model that will take its place. For now, the one-time greats of the banking world may aptly be compared with former heavyweight boxing champions of whom it is famously said: 'They never come back!'

The reason why the two antagonists ultimately stuck it out with each other for 130 years is obvious. One camp could not make do without the equity strength of the bank as a whole in cases of crisis, or without the other's customer contacts. The other camp, meanwhile, proudly pointed to their gold-rimmed annual accounts, which were not based by coincidence on good stock market years. But for the bank as a whole, demonstratively holding on to power was the prime consideration, true to the motto 'Unity is strength'.

When the stock markets decimate corporate shares to such disastrous effect, however, and the situation shows no sign of improving, there is good reason to fear for a company's restoration to former glory. Whoever thinks it is enough to wait for the good times to return knowingly ignores factors such as the dramatic fall in population over the last 20 years, and the greatly reduced industrial growth, triggered by the European Stability Pact of Maastricht and Amsterdam which imposed a collective limit on debt.

Both trends are sufficient to bring a worldwide paradigm change to the banking and financial markets, in all likelihood ending once and for all a 50-year period of growth. A scenario of this kind is still left out of analyses. Clearly, no one wishes to dramatize the situation by expressly broaching this development.

The universal banking system under ideological suspicion

It was said at the beginning of this chapter that every ideology fulfils a certain function, namely of replacing a reality deficit that is hard to bear with a plausible and self-confirming explanation. Ideology makes the claim of being able to interpret reality in a very certain way. Something that is believed to confirm this in no uncertain terms is the fact that the majority of the public inclines to subscribe to the interpretation 'One hundred million Americans can't be wrong', or that the issue in question has always been explained this way and no other.

The exponents of the universal banking system typically draw on a mixture of several ideologies:

- the fairy tale of a universally deployable set of banking instruments drawn from the roots of a national banking industry
- the fairy tale of a universally deployable classification system to register cultural differences worldwide
- the 'gullible' customer's echo as 'feedback' to the omnipotent public image promoted by the universal banks
- the universal banks' self-fixated self-indoctrination in promoting their public image
- the infatuation of a national public with the belief that its banking system is perfect – as 'feedback' to the self-image of the system as the universal standard, plausibile and feasibile for undertakings.

The interpretation of being stricken by ideology as partial blindness to reality seems to stand in bizarre contrast to the professional ability of experienced bankers to analyse all kinds of risks. In fact, this appraisal of risks is as a rule confined to the analysis of objects; one's own standpoint is excluded, and it is precisely this fact that is the cause of this failure to recognize reality.

What one has to notice is a general lapse in thinking concerning the difference between the overall strategic interests of the universal bank as such on one hand and the strategic interests resulting from the numerous banking products. What this means is the difference between actual contingency and the broad, figurative sense his fact of life directly affects the possibilities of existence of the great universal banks in the long run.

Notes

1. T. Geiger, *Ideology und Wahrheit* (Stuttgart, Vienna: Humboldt Verlag, 1953).
2. M. Pohl, *Entstehung und Entwicklung des Universalbankensystems – Konzentration und Krise als wichtige Faktoren* (Frankfurt: Fritz Knapp Verlag, 1986).
3. H. E. Büschgen, *Universalbanken oder spezialisierte Banken als Ordnungsalternativen für das Bankgewerbe der Bundesrepublik Deutschland* (Cologne, 1970).
4. W. Engels, *Der Kapitalismus und seine Krisen* (Düssezdorf: Schäfer – Poeschez Verlag, 1996).

12
The Problem with the Presence of Commercial Banks Abroad

Difference between operative and strategic planning

In order to visualize the process of planning new branch establishments and the strategies by which they are to be run, one must first differentiate between operative planning and strategic planning. Operative planning proceeds from the success potentials available and tries to anticipate short- and medium-term success by way of hard, quantitative facts in the form of costs, returns, business volumes and so on. Strategic planning, on the other hand, is intended to help develop principles with which new potentials are in future to be built up and safeguarded, thereby improving the bank's prospects of gain on a lasting basis. The emphasis here is placed on qualitative measuring techniques such as opportunities, threats, dependencies, synergies and success potentials.

Essence of corporate strategy in banking

Meyer[1] argues that a bank stipulates the following in its corporate strategy:

- the sectors in which it wishes to operate and secure its survival
- the social groups (customers, capital providers, employees and other groups) the bank has in mind
- the abilities it would like to develop in order to develop and exploit lasting competitive advantages and synergy effects
- the technologies, (in particular, information and communications technology) it wishes to use
- the allocation of personnel and financial resources
- the criteria to be applied to gauge changes in the bank's competitive position.

Seen as a whole, the bank's future position may also be described in terms of capability: what types of services it intends to offer to cater effectively to the needs of certain customer groups in the various markets, thereby offering services distinctly recognizable from those provided by rivals.

Conceivable strategy levels in banking

These consist of the following:

- the level of strategic business units
- the level of the functional areas
- the level of the bank as a whole
- the level of the bank's associates
- the level of banking groups
- the level of the industry as such.

Systematics of strategic success factors

Strategic success factors are to be understood as influencing factors on which the success of a credit institution causally depends. They are normally broken down into two groups: success factors of attractive markets, and success factors of relative competitive strength. This chapter is devoted solely to the success factors of attractive markets.

The strategic success factors of the attractiveness of markets describe markets and target groups in which the bank is active, or might become active. The more attractive such a market potential appears, the more important it appears to the bank to become active in that market. Since it is possible that rival banks could come to the same conclusion, the probability exists that competitors might take up business in this market first.

Strategic success factors of the attractiveness of markets are considered to be:

- market potential
- the competitive situation
- the general economic, legal and political situation
- formal customer behaviour
- the potential for rationalization
- the assertable price level.

Together, these different success factors make up the overall success position which a bank holds in a certain field of business. The strategic success factors of the attractiveness of markets constitute, in terms of the outer environment, the conditions for success in the specific business field. These are conditions that the bank itself cannot influence, and mark the attractiveness of a market not only for the bank scrutinizing the market but also for the competitors who are either already active in that market or who are considering entering it. They can be identified as follows.

1 Of particular significance in this context is the market potential, meaning the maximum number of customers, each with different potential demands, that may be reached by the bank.
2 The competitive situation may be such that, for example, competition in this market segment is not too tough at present, but a bank entering the market today may keep other competitors from taking the plunge tomorrow.
3 When it comes to officially justifying such a step externally, the general economic, legal and political situation is undoubtedly of considerable political importance when assessing the attractiveness of a market.
4 If the foreign market under observation is a country with which scarcely any relations have been maintained to date, the position is altogether different inasmuch as the bank in question has a pioneering role to perform for the entire international banking community. This gives rise to the 'enviable' reputation of being the first to take the plunge.
5 The expression 'formal customer behaviour' refers to the special forms of behaviour banking customers usually demonstrate towards providers, meaning whether needs are usually met with one provider (principal banker) or selectively with a number of providers; and also whether the modes of behaviour of banking customers are to be considered as critical, open-minded, price-conscious and willing to cooperate, or querulous.
6 A market's rationalization potential indicates the extent to which opportunities still exist to raise even further the effectiveness of production and sales by rationalizing. In the 1990s, a number of leading banks from industrial nations believed foreign markets to contain such rationalization potential. Since they felt themselves capable of lowering local production and distribution costs on a lasting basis, they allowed themselves to be tempted – on the basis solely of this calculation – to set up a branch of their own. The other potential competitors interpreted this decision as proof that this was a step well worth taking and, in cases of doubt, worthy of imitation. The important thing was to be a little smarter, more purposeful and faster than those before. Such a decision could then be presented to one's own public as proof of having caught up with the vanguard of renowned and progressive institutions.

Experience has taught us that when a bank enters the market in a new region, high fixed costs are involved. The biggest cost items are setting up the base and developing one's own sales channel with a permanent staff capable of communicating with the home market and its corporate clients, and this requirement involves more than overcoming the language barrier.

Misinterpretation of locally available data

Informative though the studies by consultants may be (also with regard to foreign banking markets), grave methodological reservations should be called for regarding the usefulness of such information as a basis for a foreign bank's decision to enter a market.

Usually, what happens is that sparse information on the target country's banking sector is 'stretched' by taking a hypothetically increased number of competitors. From there, possible market shares are calculated. The procedure applied, then, is the 'as if method', which plays down the information deficit that actually exists.

Foreign activities at a general disadvantage

To illustrate the difference between domestic market activities and foreign market activities from the operational point of view, it is useful to bear in mind the strengths, meaning the factors determining success, of a banking activity based in a domestic market or region:

- a culturally homogeneous customer base, thanks to the width, density and depth of the territory
- the willingness on the part of customers to resort, as a rule, to the same old bank to meet a considerable part of its banking needs.

The interplay between these two principles – customer proximity in sales and the customers' willingness to have their overall banking needs catered for out of a wide range of products and services – guarantees, on the basis of the homogeneous numbers of services offered, an optimal combination of strategic success factors, for only in this constellation do the principles for success (economies of scale thanks to a given critical mass of customers, synergies between business fields and a break-even point when fixed costs are covered) take effect.

When a bank enters a foreign market, however, hardly any of these profitability-supporting ratios prove effective. This is why a foreign presence, wherever its location, must from the outset be viewed in a negative light in terms of costs.

Note

1. H. Meyer zu Selhausen, *Bank-Informationssysteme – Eine Bankbetriebswirtschaftslehre mit IT-Schwerpunkt* (Stuttgart: Schäffer–Poeschez–Verlag, 2000) p. 415.

13
The 'Domestic–Foreign' Conflict as Multiple Cultural Interference Factor

Services and goods production as opposites

As has been implied in connection with the antitrust law procedure, the special nature of banking is, in principle, not covered by the usual technocratic categorization within a global economic policy classification scheme in which all commercial phenomena are 'treated equally' in terms of legislation and regulation. As a result, banking is considered as being the 'production' of services and is tossed into one pot along with the production and marketing of manufactured goods.

Seen from the sociological viewpoint, this is misleading, particularly with respect to cross-border business, as manufactured goods do not acquire their needs-oriented significance until they are marketed. They obtain their utility value from the national market of end-consumers; their geographical origin is of little concern. Banking services, on the other hand, flourish like plants in a certain local environment and can rarely – irrespective of the geological sub-soil, neighbouring plants and climate – be transplanted anywhere else. Banks, in terms of their cultural nature, are somehow always indigenous. This being so, the blanket term 'banking products', which unfortunately has become established in the science of business economics, is unhelpful, as it tells us little about how they materialize and about the typical conditions for their reproduction.

For this reason, one can hardly speak of exporting banking products – whereby market shares are measured and categorized within a uniform classification scheme of market-predominating companies and market access criteria – as one can of exporting goods. That a formal 'equal treatment' makes little sense is demonstrated by the fact that in a national banking sector, competitive strength can be 'felt' to exist with market shares of 3 to 5 per cent, while in the case of goods it is unlikely to be much below 30 per cent.

The isolated nature of cultures is the main difficulty in the international sector

As a cultural phenomenon of the first order, a national banking system constitutes in its respective domestic sector a highly differentiated, changing entity. Viewed from without, however, it makes a very static impression. Wholly self-referring, it appears immobile and indifferent to what is going on around it. Its main characteristic is a tendency to shut itself off from the outside world as much as possible for, given its highly differentiated functionality internally, a self-referring social system that is subjected to the internal pressure of constantly having to reproduce itself has no alternative other than to project a homogeneous outer surface, if only as protection against outside influences, such as comparisons or being called into question.

The impression outsiders have of banks, then, is that they are disinterested, cold and distant. Their insular, self-absorbed nature is in keeping with their sole validity claim: namely, the self-commitment to create, internally, perfect conditions for functioning.

From this it becomes clear why systems of this kind stand in the way of an exchange with another country by erecting relatively high legal and social barriers, and why – in terms of entering into a potential cooperation or coalition – they might be said to get in their own way. According to the cultural laws under which they have entered the field, they ultimately have little alternative to this totally self-fixated attitude. Since this mode of behaviour is driven by a strong inner need to act in such a manner, and in such a manner only, outside observers have no choice other than to respect them in this sense.[1]

The secret of culture as a system is founded on its relationship to the spatial, in the relationship of social groups to the space we feel to be ours, our home, as opposed to the other that is situated outside and is felt to be foreign or alien. It is on this fundamental difference between identity and alterity, between one's home country and a foreign country, that our limited human sense of orientation in an exceedingly chaotic world is ultimately based.

Indeed, the process of self-constitution consists in constantly isolating oneself and distancing oneself from what is alien. He who sets himself apart stands on one side. Alien is, to put it generally, everyone or everything that is on the other side. Nevertheless, in distancing oneself from what is alien, this is paradoxically possible only by referring to what is alien. This means that the previously gained, insufficient information about it is again passed on as information (a thoroughly imperfect state of affairs).

National identity makes individuals act towards outside influences according to the general line of their own culture, which is to say to grasp given distinctions, superordinations and subordinations and, where necessary, to confirm them. But it is also conceivable that individuals consciously present themselves in a different manner, and that they set about launching a 'charm offensive' to put the attractiveness of their own culture to the test. They deliberately present a big-hearted, tolerant image of themselves that is, outwardly, open and accessible, and endeavours to level out any outward discrepancies that might exist. It would not be wrong to assume this eagerness to appeal to others to be the driving force behind the ambitions of large banks to expand abroad.

Be that as it may, the normal cultural self-perception and self-evaluation is likely to return in competitive stress situations, in the fight for one's very existence, and will ultimately lead to a stronger polarization of what is one's own and what is alien. In cases of doubt, one tends to consider one's own identity superior and that of the other inferior; and, according to the principle of the 'barbaric' in the ancient world, the boundaries are ultimately drawn between order and chaos or between good and bad, or between what is useful and what is not.

An important role when drawing these boundaries is played by one's perception and, above all, the (qualified) assessment of what is different. The phenomena of 'boundary' and 'crossing the boundary' are by all means complementary in terms of differentiating between what is 'one's own' and what is 'alien' inasmuch as correlations exist between the different forms that are perceived across the boundary. These may be articulated as good neighbourly relations or as a world of animosity. Such patterns of perception correspond to certain (unconscious) integration, demarcation and selection strategies.

Language boundaries as boundaries to understanding

Languages perform both an including and an excluding function. Those who speak the language belong to the group, while those who do not are excluded. Internationally distributed languages have these two functions. As the medieval language of the Church, Latin united clerical elites of different cultures while excluding, within the cultures of the national languages, the laymen. The use of English in modern communication between cultures has a similar function in that only certain elites have access to this language.

A language boundary becomes, through the formation of consciousness, a boundary to understanding when it is standardized as the national language under the influence of government authorities and strengthened by a politically drawn border. This is often also the case when there was originally no boundary.

Relatively homogeneous customer groups develop as a result of national language and legal cultures. But what is their specific needs culture? The customer adviser of a foreign bank manages to form some kind of picture of his foreign customers' interests, but he often has difficulty making sense of their financing habits and business strategies, and fitting them into a homogeneous form of reporting or control in a foreign corporate group.

For this reason, the ability to 'read' and interpret the specific requirements and expectations of certain customer groups is not a criterion for success that employees abroad can readily satisfy.

Special meaning of 'cultural differences' in service industries

According to the usage of multicultural production firms there exists a well established stock of terms for cross-cultural communication skills and functioning which a successful foreign manager should master when dealing with cultural handicaps and limitations. A standard book, such as that by Harris and Moran,[2] seems to serve quite well the needs of multicultural manufacturing businesses based on such stable classifications.

Contrary to this fact, service industries have to face basically different business conditions. The latter are dominated by conflicting cultural processes, being interlocked and developing non-stop simultaneously and in parallel to each other, so that the cultural differences appear always according to a series of perpetually changing situations. The isolated and self-absorbed nature of the cultural systems involved inevitably provokes endless kaleidoscopic situations with tensions varying according to movements in their environment. This common quality of being isolated is the reason why each culture has its own distinctive nature and dignity. This dignity is, for instance, unavoidably affected when, by the arbitrary designation of an official *lingua franca*, a feeling of humiliation is provoked.

Dealing with such situation-related judgements, their specific dramatic impact cannot be ignored even if the matter is constantly interpreted by well defined intercultural terms. Thus, the more one becomes familiarized with this kind of situation-related interplay the more one can be aware of the fact of how strange one's own position must sometimes appear from other ethnical standpoints.

One's own and the alien: the natural position of the foreign customer

Before entering into an international strategic alliance, the prospective partners must ascertain whether mutual interests exist that may serve as a basis for embarking upon a joint undertaking. This would involve examining the cultural boundaries of the two poles of the respective banking system drawn *vis-à-vis* each other and the possibility of networking the two banks' operating systems. Further, it is appropriate to analyse the structural compatibility of both partners' organizations as well as customers' expectations in third countries where these come into consideration as a joint target group.

This gives rise to certain key questions: is it possible in principle to conduct commercial banking with foreign customers in the same way as with domestic customers? Or is it appropriate, in the light of the unusual forms business activities take in guest countries, to judge them according to the criteria of the country of origin? Can one assume that foreign customers are willing and able to focus constantly on two different national systems to such an extent that they are capable, say, of negotiating compromises as constructions for a special purpose?

The latter is unlikely to be the case. Instead, potential customers in the guest country will, when in doubt, confine themselves entirely to their domestic view of things and will want to exclude elements that appear alien. In short, they will attach importance to being judged and treated in the manner customary in their own country and not according to certain values and standardizations derived from the position of the USA qualified as a 'universal standarization' for such matters.

Consequently, a foreign branch will arouse keen interest on the part of a potential customer only if the latter already maintains a concrete business relationship with the bank's country of origin. In all other cases, a foreign bank's offer of services will be disregarded from the outset. Absolutely no notice will be taken of it.

National banking cultures as doctrinaire powers

Human communities form closed, self-regulating systems. Characteristic of these systems is the degree of openness and consistency that underlies their identity in each case, which is the result of permanent boundary selections whereby various elements and sectors are linked and made to communicate. Without the boundary selection mechanism there would be chaos.

In keeping with the specific 'more or less' of openness via inclusions and exclusions, the respective conditions for being given access to, or membership in, social systems make up an interrelated complex of patterns of action and understanding, including such practices as, for example, business practices or education practices. The more complex and predominant such practices appear, the stronger is the tendency for these practices to gradually become life-styles or work-styles.

Combinations of relatively homogeneous spatial and temporal bundles of ways of acting and understanding can give rise to even more complex forms that may, as a national work-style, become the personification of an entire social sector or business. Repeated and completed by generation after generation, they become the binding, typified self-image.[5]

From this may be derived, in turn, a topology of one's own and the alien which conveys to the individual specific identification patterns as if to say: 'You're not just different from me; you are where I can't be without becoming someone else. If I were where you are, I would not be me.'[6]

Anyone who has ever experienced from the inside how foreign banking systems work in theory and in practice knows the great importance placed by the national training institutions on uniformly defined teaching with regard to the use of specialist terminology and symbols and, based on those, procedures in the sense of uniformly stipulated knowledge. Precise compliance with them is necessary, if only to safeguard quality in banking.

Under the German 'dual education system', for example, hundreds of vocational school teachers and thousands of trainers watch over the uniform education of trainees to ensure the precise usage of the official specialist language, a vital prerequisite if a banking system based on a division of labour is to function effectively. In France, banking theory is taught intensively at all regional and local levels, from technical colleges and universities to the legendary *grandes écoles*. The fact that French junior bankers must make their own way up the career ladder is possible because of the great importance attached to a sound expert knowledge.

One might refer to the local authorities which supervise the uniform use of specialist knowledge in theory and in practice as the 'border guards' of their social system, for as multipliers they reinforce both the 'purity' of expert knowledge and a credibly developed, uniform career system which is intended to grant equality of opportunity. The purpose of these continuous national measures is to provide uniform standards for practice, across all groups of institutions and regions, to enable young bankers to apply for clearly defined positions on the labour market that allow them little time to adjust to their new tasks.

Yet this 'national banking culture' not only has this vibrant interior teeming with specialist knowledge but also – as has been said several times above – a relatively stand-offish, disinterested exterior. In analogy to the theory of evolution in biology one might assume a certain inherent law to exist in this context: on the 'active side' a refinement of performance has been achieved, while on the 'passive side' there is – in reverse proportion – a reduced ability to adapt. The resultant tendency to isolate oneself is reflected in a limited perceptive faculty externally and in a permanent compulsion to defend oneself and justify one's actions in terms of one's own national standpoint. Every innovation that is fashioned after a model from abroad has difficulty being accepted in day-to-day business at home. This is why such a process of change can only gradually (which is to say, over prolonged periods of time) be integrated into the national working methodology.

Given this difficult 'passive side' to national working cultures, and not only in banking, it is not surprising that prior to the BNP–Dresdner experiment there was no predecessor in terms of international strategic alliances, and neither – despite the fact that the European banking market is now a reality – is there likely to be another such experiment any time soon.

Homo-polar intercultural factors repel

We have already seen that intercultural fields of tension arise, as a rule, from differences between the interior and the exterior as well as from the outward isolation of cultures. These inherent laws have their roots in the cultural steering of human nature, and are always present in one way or another when different nationally coloured experiences are triggered by historical occurrences. However, it is quite conceivable that these factors may be overlapped by a third component which has a similar impact on both sides, a component with a dual effect that attracts attention and makes a lasting impression. An international ideology which establishes itself in the thinking of both sides is most certainly capable of lastingly suppressing motivation on both sides. In other words, thought and action, the identification of interests and of priorities of action may – by way of subtle restrictions and dissociations – create obstacles in the joint working process at any time.

The universal banking ideology, intensified to the absolute, does have a dominant effect on the representatives of the schools of thought of both nationalities. Each side presumes it possesses the ability to categorize and appreciate all phenomena with true objectivity; it is the latter that makes coordination across national borders so terribly difficult. The purpose of such coordination lies in the transformation of claims to competence (which essentially scarcely differ from one another) into concrete joint positions, and in creating from these a basis for motivation for further joint activities.

In endeavouring to determine in what way such a homo-polar fundamental constellation can affect the attempt by two universal banks with a similar strategic profile to establish a cross-border strategic alliance, one cannot help but see in the homo-polarity a fundamental socio-cultural deficit, a 'birth defect', for the strategic alliance in question.

This deficit is the main cause of a latently perceptible unwillingness to cooperate that is difficult to remedy in the long run. It also explains the phenomenon whereby vanity can render one partner incapable of admitting that they really need the other for their own self-realization. Seen from this angle, the alliance takes on the quality of an extravagant luxury. This luxury is part of a certain view that perfectionist advocates of the universal banking ideology find extremely difficult to admit to. Then, at an advanced stage, partners to an alliance often succumb to a strange jealousy of the shared 'baby' (the independent institutions given like by the alliance).

The cooperation project is dealt a further blow by the wait-and-see tactics resorted to on both sides, and assumes a somewhat ghostly air when both players act as if the game had not yet started ('Brussels apparently has yet to make its decision!'), and as if all that mattered for now was to adapt the non-committal pose of the perfect candidate, for the rest casting about for suitable excuses as to why this was hardly the right time for a decisive course of action.

The above examples show that a constructive starting point for a transnational strategic alliance can be presumed to exist only after a development phase in which one's absolute faith in the universal banking ideology has been well and truly shaken. Only then will it be truly possible to 'strike out for new shores', as only 100 per cent commitment can guarantee that the status quo will really be changed. Thus the credibility of a cooperation project hinges on certain indications that the parties concerned are serious about wanting to create an innovative basis for their operations. When a majority takeover has been made or a large-scale merger is scheduled, everyone is immediately clear about the seriousness of the situation. With a strategic alliance, all that may initially be expected is a great deal of political hot air and wait-and-see tactics.

One sign that a serious development was under way would be if the players were actually able to convey the impression that the potential brought in by the respective partner opened up for them totally new opportunities and prospects, and that they were willing to do everything to exploit these possibilities without delay. Only when one partner learns from the other that the latter is absolutely dependent on the alliance for their own self-realization is there any chance of ending this waiting game. If the only aim is to occupy a possible preliminary stage of the cooperation to this end, it will be difficult to generate the requisite credibility.

This fact underlines, moreover, the enormous difference that exists between corporate alliances or mergers in the services sector and the manufacturing sector. In the latter case, the place where the construction blueprints come from, components are produced, assembly is carried out and the person responsible for marketing is, generally speaking, of no significance in its success or otherwise. In the services sector, on the other hand, not only is location all-important, but success also hinges to a great extent on individuals as well as (where potential customers are concerned) on credibility. Without these factors, doing business at an international level is out of the question.

Practical principles for international cooperation

As has been said, intercultural fields of tension come about when cultures that are isolated from each other come into contact. Since cultures, as complex social systems, have to reproduce themselves constantly, they tend to remain stable over lengthy periods of time. Little change has been made to the cultural boundaries of Europe since the migration of nations ended in the first millennium. These boundaries only became more pronounced with the appearance of nation states in the second millennium. At the beginning of the third, the question to be asked now is: as globalization advances, are there any prospects that these tensions may be substantially reduced? If there were, they could be seen as a glimmer of hope that greater importance would be given to transnational strategic alliances in the future.

However, hopes of this kind are deceptive, as cultural phenomena make themselves felt regardless of the currents of fashion. When one isolates oneself, phenomena are perceived in a distorted manner.

To put it another way, transnational concepts can withstand the over-whelming power of partner cultures and retain their bridge-building function where a clear-cut concept has been drawn up. Given that projects of this kind are bound to draw fire, as it were, it is important to wait for the counter-reactions they produce and face up to them, rather than rely on evasive tactics to avoid anticipated difficulties; experience shows that this would only aggravate such difficulties. Seen in this light, a project conducted across national borders can only be deemed to have prospects of future success if a high degree of precision is achieved and the temptation to resort to imprecise phrases that do not have to be explained until some later time can be withstood.

As a contrast to domestic cooperation projects, a cross-border project cannot expect to 'run under its own steam' after a certain start-up time. Metaphorically speaking, managing cross-border projects is like transporting things by boat against the current, full steam ahead and without let-up. With domestic business it is possible to 'go with the flow' and put one's trust in the hope that things will settle down at some point. But if the boat headed up-river at some point lacks the steam to stay on course, it will immediately be caught by domestic currents and pushed in the direction of domestic business. Only in the safe waters of domestic business is there a chance of 'keeping an even keel' merely by following routine.

Imprecise phrases or expressions that need to be specified within a certain period of time are makeshift solutions; they offer little prospect of actually buying time.

Principles of success for transnational alliances

These include the following elements.

1 A master plan, with specific objectives and contents, is an absolute prerequisite.
2 The implementation of the master plan is – for reasons of credibility – a purpose in itself and not a means of fulfilling some other purpose.
3 Parts of the project to be carried out consecutively should follow a previously agreed timetable.
4 The project should not be started until objectives have been sufficiently established.
5 Setting up findings committees is unsuitable for finalizing points if results are to be achieved under pressure of time.
6 Rotating committee meetings foster the procrastination of decisions that cannot be put off.
7 Decision-making committees whose members are appointed according to the principle of parity are inefficient. Stalemate situations are the result, and too many problems are disregarded because everything has to be done on the basis of the lowest common denominator.

8   Dualistic tendencies must be curbed by establishing specific actions.
9   Pleasant-sounding declarations of intent usually have an 'alibi' function.
10 The creation of new words is appropriate when thought-provoking impulses with a transnational slant have to be communicated.
11 Managerial responsibility should be indivisible and assigned to individuals (if possible, individuals from outside).
12 The transnational project manager is like the conductor of an orchestra who conveys a uniform picture of the score.
13 The cornerstone of PR work is transparency – also transparency of difficulties – towards a knowledgeable and interested public that is willing to be understanding.
14 Dialogue with antitrust authorities helps prevent legends and myths ('power of international banks').
15 The phrase 'equal rights' should be replaced by 'equal obligations'.
16 Communication internally and externally should not be hampered by prescribed, official language.

Closing appraisal of the BNP–Dresdner experiment

In the light of the above cultural-sociological insights it should be possible to look back to the strategic alliance between BNP and Dresdner Bank and ask why the revolutionary, transnational intentions the project was launched with were, from the intercultural viewpoint, doomed to failure from the first. Indeed, after roughly five years, a point was reached at which the confidence which had been placed in the vision of a cross-border alliance was exhausted in both national banking cultures. Things then went the way they must, despite desperate efforts by the managements of both banks to again avert the verdict of the outcome of the experiment.

From then on, there was clearly no longer any chance that this daring undertaking would prove itself after all. The fact that each of the two banks had held a prominent status, a certain key position, in their respective banking sectors was no longer an adequate reason to believe they might 'pull it off'. The sole question that remained was this: 'Does it work or does it not?'

This question referred to the heart of the experiment, namely the bringing together of units from both banks to form a joint holding company in order to achieve a fusion of the French with the German banking culture by degrees, thereby establishing a truly European big bank. The idea to begin with was to create the conditions for a regular merger of the two banks, first in third countries and then on a European scale. But would this have posed a threat to the continued existence of their two banking cultures? Probably not. Nevertheless, this was – psychologically speaking – the all-important point that inescapably came to test the mettle of the two national banking systems.

The issue of how this specific project would be completed had not yet been contractually agreed upon. The final arrangements were to have been set down in an additional agreement, and work would have been started on it immediately the partners agreed on the location and nationality of the seat of the holding company. This, it turned later out, was little more than a trick.

When, from mid-1995, it became obvious that there was not going to be any such agreement, the partners tried via their 'Plan B' (Alliance II) to at least find a face-saving solution for the cooperation. At this point, the inability by the two national banking cultures was plain to see. An inability to follow the experiment of an international strategic alliance with such far-reaching consequences had spread, quietly, on both sides. How was this attitude to be recognized? It became apparent when 'old hands', recognized experts in international business who had hitherto followed the experiment with interest, increasingly asked: 'Own up: does it really work?' This was a sign that the negative outcome was, as it were, official. For the shamans of both systems it was now clear that the further-reaching objectives of the alliance were unfeasible. It looked as though the revolutionary experiment as it had originally been envisaged, and whose electrifying myth had fired the public's imagination, would never be successful.

The fathers of the agreement had tried as a precautionary measure to side-step the critical point by a trick: that is, by switching the decisive criterion for success to a third country. The legal principles that would apply to the holding company were to be taken neither from the French nor from the German banking and legal culture, but from that of a third country that was to be the pivot of the entire experiment. By resorting to this roundabout solution, neither party was ultimately – seemingly – in the wrong, yet the prospects of the success of the project had been violated. Thus, everything was to be played out in all innocence according to the rules of this third country no one had identified.

What, basically, the alliance would have had to achieve would have been to build a strong bridge between the two banking cultures, thereby providing competitors with a shining example to follow. If only because of the additional problems it would have created, the third-country solution could never have fulfilled such a bridge function.

The central question – in retrospect, of course – is this: could the experiment have been saved by deciding on a location for the holding company at an early stage, on the merits of the legal system of one of the two partner countries? This would have been the legal system that provided the most favourable taxation solution for the holding company. As was seen later when Hoechst and Rhône-Poulenc merged to form Novartis, this would probably have been the French taxation regime. What would the arguments have been at that time against choosing Strasbourg as the location? Might the fact that the Alsatian city was not considered an international stock exchange centre have proved a disadvantage to the project in our age of electronic cross-border trading systems? If not, what prevented BNP and Dresdner from reaching this conclusion?

They lacked the courage to state openly the objectives of the strategic alliance, including the option of a merger at some future point in time. A certain absence of faith gave rise to a lack of courage to propose a forward-looking solution to the respective banks' national public in the way that was seemingly possible with the merger of Hoechst AG and Rhône-Poulenc, in the case of which share ownership was similarly widespread. The French banking system cannot have been a hindrance, France having officially introduced universal banking in 1984. Further, the monopoly of the *agents de change* in securities trading was abolished in 1986. Were there any other reasons to shy away from such a solution? Surely not.

By electing to hide themselves behind the alibi of a third-country solution for the holding company, the management of Dresdner at that time squandered a momentous opportunity. Had not, at the same time, the German federal government and the German Bundestag (lower house) declared themselves in favour – following German reunification – of introducing the euro as Europe's single currency, thereby setting a glowing example of how to bravely and self-confidently disregard the national ire at thoughts of losing the Deutschmark in order to secure the future of Europe (and, with that, of Germany)?

Of course, intercultural obstacles such as the 'birth defect' of the similarity of structure and the attitude of rejection on the part of the banking cultures would, as has been described above, have caused great difficulties. But such misgivings were not articulated. Instead, the partner banks – like Laocoön and his sons – allowed themselves to be worn down by the 'snakes' (run of events) in a long-drawn exhibition contest, hoping all the while to score a few points for their 'performance'.

Strictly speaking, this undertaking does not deserve the term 'experiment'. At best, it may be described as a 'pseudo experiment' with some theatricals thrown in for good measure. The feasibility of the venture had not by any stretch of the imagination been sufficiently analysed and secured, and so the idea shared by the two banks should not have been fed to the press as early as it was.

Alliance II was a different matter. In that it was restricted to a joint monoculture in eastern Europe, it constituted a serious attempt not only to save face but also to assume some responsibility for economic development there, a fact that customers in eastern Europe honoured for a good decade. Developments subsequently no longer ran according to plan, and the project had to be abandoned. But it gave both partners useful insights into business conditions in those reforming countries, which later served as a basis for the business activities pursued in that region by each bank on its own. Thus, invaluable experience was gained there that contributed towards the further expansion of the close relations between BNP and Dresdner Bank. The future developments of banking in Europe will decide whether this relationship is continued further, and according to whatever set of circumstances is then prevailing.

Notes

1. Quite another impression prevails among those who follow, through the media, international developments and related attempts at conflict-solving. Because the main focus is always on international activities in politics and economics, the natural tendency is to consider this sector a primarily political, formable dimension of universal validity. There is, unfortunately, little room for intercultural misunderstandings and the human inability properly to shape relations to the outside world in the superficiality of this view of the world. For this reason, imperfection in this sector can, for them, be nothing but a regrettable relic of bygone days, because it does not compare with our idealized world of progress. But how is one to explain the fact that in our globalized world of progress it has so far been impossible in the 50 years of international European communities, today known as the European Union, to establish a European public worthy of the name? Has this not to do with the member states' latent rejection of self-regulating social systems? No matter how much they may celebrate their membership outwardly, they would rather distance themselves from it in cases of doubt. How is a common European public to evolve under these circumstances?
2. Philip R. Harris and Robert T. Moran, 'Managing Cultural Differences (Houston, TX: Gulf, 1991), 3rd ed.
3. For more about the relationship between globalization and identity see George Schöpflin, Frankfurter Rundschau, October 16th 1999, "Ein Gefühl der Demütigung".
4. The concept of intercultural performance has its implied limits. By cross-cultural experiences one can obviously increase the exchanges, satisfy one's curiosity about the other, multiply contacts and finally construct an atmosphere of confidence. Insofar as developing cultural awareness and understanding is concerned, it is basically a matter of open-mindedness and of high standards in human relations. It does not necessarily have a direct impact on the organization, even if it is true that a good organization facilitates the development of intercultural projects. (cf. J. Bachèlerie Les Cahiers, No 9, September 1998, p. 52.
5. G. Ammon, Der französische Wirtschaftsstil (Munich: Eberhard, 1989).
6. B. Waldenfels, 'Schwellenerfahrung und Grenzziehung', in M. Fludernik and H. J. Gehrke (eds), Grenzgänger zwischen Kulturen (Würzburg: Ergon, 1999).

14

Outlook: Are International Strategic Alliances More Likely in the Post-universal Banking Era?

Will reducing the universal banking principle be a problem?

Our examination has shown that the image of the universal bank has passed through a number of historical changes and been influenced by various factors. The question as to whether it may in principle be reduced can be answered as follows: something that has grown over the course of time can degenerate during a process of contraction, but the question is whether it is still the same thing? If so, the falseness of the claim to being a provider of all-embracing, universal expertise becomes blatantly obvious. The result is of a different order.

Assuming there is such a thing as an unmistakable core of universal bank elements, however, one might still speak of the same species in spite of a contraction process. There is a case for both viewpoints. When changes are to be made at traditional universal banks, therefore, there is no need to question their old identity. But when – as a result of a merger, say – newly formed big banks are given an organization and strategy geared to modern-day requirements, we find ourselves dealing with something else.

The universal bank originated in the nineteenth century from the strategic objective of setting up and operating an all-embracing financial system for a growing economy, unhindered by government restrictions. After each bank had got off to an individual start, more and more uniform traits were developed. Gradually, however, the influencing role passed to the customers, who developed their own expectations and grew increasingly sophisticated in their demands. Concerned for their profile, the banks subsequently endeavoured to underscore their claims to essentially unlimited expertise as principal banker by constantly coming up with innovative services, the aim of which was to safeguard or enhance prestige.

Generally speaking, it is possible to distinguish four stages which have since become permanent features of the universal bank.

1 The systemization of bank services in corporate banking as principal bankers providing a comprehensive spectrum of products.
2 The strong demand for bank loans between the two world wars in the absence of functioning financial markets.
3 In times of above-average economic growth after the Second World War, as ever-greater use was made of data processing and deposits became, (and remained) more expensive, the universal banks embarked upon a broad-based expansion into retail business.
4 Faced with real or imagined limits to growth at home, the universal banks sought from the mid-1980s to expand their operations abroad, where they remained in competition with one another.

The overall development of three decades came to a head in gigantic accumulations of staff-intensive organizational forms, which explains why the presence of the banks was ten times greater than in the nineteenth century. The ideas of omnipotence and omnipresence, which became the foremost features of a large bank's strategy, are a reflection of how banks saw themselves. All it then took was the absolute completion of their product range and their strategic self-reference as global players to justify 'membership' in an exclusive 'club' of the world's leading banks. As protagonists of an industrial modern age they felt themselves nothing short of predestined, not only to exploit this potential to the full but also to expand it further wherever possible in order to achieve growth targets on their own resources, which is to say without third-party involvement.

In reply to the above question about whether the prospects of international strategic alliances will be better in a post-universal banking era, the answer will very much depend on whether the tendency we have witnessed to become fixated with the glorification of the perfection of their own power persists, or whether in the current banking crisis signs are to be found of a new mentality in terms of an ability and a willingness to enter into a cooperation.

The 'all-embracing' universal banking principle and its gradual detachment from reality

The discovery that the operative apparatus the universal banks had built up over the previous 20 years, with all its expansions from the previous decades, could be justified only if economic growth continued caused, on the verge of the twenty-first century, the top executives of the universal banks to shudder. All of a sudden, this growth could no longer be expected to last. Apparently they had overlooked the fact that demographic growth had already been in a state of decline for two decades, and that this trend would continue unabated.

The fact that the EU member countries had committed themselves under the 1997 Stability Pact of Amsterdam to observe absolute monetary discipline, resulting in an extremely low level of interest rates with a flat interest rate curve and minimum revenues from maturity transformation in lending operations, further accelerated this new interest rate trend. The ensuing new economic situation requires all participants in the economic process, including the banks, to produce new answers to the paradigm change taking place. Even disregarding loan losses, it is unclear how banks are in future to cover their unavoidably high fixed costs given this large number of lines of business (some of which are loss-making). Continuing as before is no longer an option.

What is more, particularly in international commercial banking, there has been a trend for quite some time now whereby multinational companies refrain from calling on the banks' intermediary services, and instead cover their financing and investment needs on their own, within the group. Since they already know where the funds are to come from and how they will be employed, liquidity equalization within the group can be far less costly than the services provided by banks, whose information management forces them to take all kinds of possible constellations into consideration from the outset. On the international financial markets, the multinationals have almost drawn level with the banks in any case where the issuance of their own debt securities is concerned. This enables them to pass the funds thus procured on to group companies in need of capital.

As we have seen, banking grew ten times as fast as the rest of the economy in the twentieth century, making sweeping action inevitable at some point to align the entire banking sector with the existing business volume. This fulfils a prophecy by Ulrich Cartellieri, a member of the Management Board of Deutsche Bank, Germany's biggest universal bank.

As early as 1991, Cartellieri had compared the structural problems awaiting the banking sector in the 1990s with the steel industry, and predicted that immense cuts would have to be made. As is well known, once protectionist trading barriers were removed in the 1970s, the steel sector saw prices fall on the world market, giving rise to vast overcapacities just about everywhere. These could only be remedied by closing down steelworks on a large scale, which in turn aggravated the already difficult labour market situation. Though often repeated, the prediction that a similar fate awaited the banking industry was taken seriously by next to no one. Attempts were launched in the late 1990s to cut jobs in a 'socially acceptable' manner, but this situation has yet to be consciously addressed by strategy.

This again demonstrates the ideological side of the universal banking principle. It will take more than inconsistencies with economic trends to refute the almost religious belief placed in the traditional superiority of universal banking as something of a national achievement. After all, macro-economic reality has never proceeded in a straight line, but in cycles (hence the belief that things would one day pick up again). To the layman, nothing serious can befall anyone whose business is with money or goods. As long as the professionals of the banking business apply the same maxim, the process of reducing staff numbers without any specific target in mind ('just in case') is likely to go on for quite some time. The trusty old principle will not be defeated so easily.

The new competitive model: 'glass banks' in keeping with Basle II

The Japanese banking crisis in the second half of the 1990s and its implications for the international financial system prompted the bank supervisory and regulatory bodies, in collaboration with the central banks via the Bank for International Settlements (BIS) in Basle, to seek an (internationally agreed) way out.

This was not the first time such action had been taken. Under the Basle Concordat of 1975 – formulated in reply to the Herstattbank crisis – cooperation was agreed on between the national bank supervisory authorities of all the industrial nations. The Basle Accord of 1988 (Basle I) finally laid down the first common minimum capital standards for banks. These standards were considered indispensable as a buffer against credit risks, and the aim was to prevent a sudden weakening in the banking sector from harming entire economies.

Since 1999, the Basle Committee has been conducting negotiations to find ways to protect against banks' insolvencies by completely revamping these requirements (Basle II). Instead of the present, undifferentiated practice of granting loans to companies of all categories and the lack of differentiation when fixing terms, the creditworthiness of the individual borrower is in future to be the sole criterion. In other words, it should not be possible for 'bad borrowers' to be 'subsidized' throughout the entire sector by the 'best borrowers'. This unfortunate state of affairs, which competition was unable to put to rights, is now to be rectified in a joint effort by all legislators and supervisory authorities.

In future, then, the outcome of the credit assessment will be the sole decisive factor in determining both the capital needed to back credit risks and pricing. Consequently, the maximum volume of loans a bank is permitted to grant will stand in direct relation to the credit quality of its borrowers. As a result, capital requirements can in future be higher or lower – depending on the credit risk – than the present, generally applicable requirement of 8 per cent of the loan amount. It is envisaged that top-rated companies will be weighted at 20 per cent, while extremely poorly rated firms would receive a weighting of 150 per cent. An average company, meanwhile, would retain its 100 per cent weighting (in terms of backing of 8 per cent).

The result of the assessment of a company's future business prospects is a rating that may be awarded either as an external rating (by private agencies) or as an internal rating (compiled by the banks themselves using refined measuring techniques). Uniformity of these internal ratings is to be guaranteed for all banks by an EU directive and its translation into national law. Particularly stringent requirements will apply to risk management and controlling in lending, and an improved risk management may bring banks 'credit points'.

Further, stricter duties concerning the disclosure of ratios are to give stock market participants important indications of how a particular bank's risk situation should be assessed. In other words, with the help of enhanced market transparency, the underlying system will put the markets in a position to punish banks that carry a greater risk with lower share price quotations and higher interest rates for the raising of funds. The aim is to encourage banks to bring their business policy into line with the market. If a lower risk in terms of the choice of the debtor is rewarded by a bigger lending volume, banks should not pass up this chance to regain their financial strength through recognition in the market.

Thus, Basle II is to create equal competitive conditions for all market participants, big and small, whether operating domestically or internationally. Without doubt, this system is bound to have an impact on the various domestic markets, but it will also have an effect across national borders. Indeed, it has every prospect of serving as a paradigm for a new era in the history of banking.

However, one may still speak of a certain inequality in the preparation stage. As some national banking industries have absolutely no experience with rating systems, there may be certain competitive disadvantages during the initial phase which starts in 2007. What debtor was so forward-looking, before the launch, as to opt voluntarily for a foreign rating system involving – particularly for medium-sized companies – not inconsiderable costs? Protectionist support measures designed to combat new developments considered by the rest of the world to be progressive can never be justified. For this reason there cannot be any way at the national level of withdrawing from the indivisibility of this worldwide system of assessing creditworthiness.

How can bank shares be a stock market success in future?

Banks run as joint stock corporations have been dependent on the grace of the stock markets and the inflow of capital since well before Basle II. Especially in times of weak earnings when it is not possible to build up reserves, their prospects for the future are in the hands of the stock market in that stock market expectations as regards the earnings power of the employed capital are an expression of clear minimum requirements.

Even when universal banking ruled supreme, relations between banks and shareholders were not exactly perfect. Particularly in Germany, the relationship was marked by the banks' condescending behaviour towards shareholders, which contrasted strongly with how they treated customers. The fear that customers might be lured away by rival institutions was infinitely greater. In normal times, finding buyers for share issues was not considered a problem. After all, banks were thought of as having the greatest possible credit quality after joint stock corporations majority-held by the government. In return, shareholders had to accept certain disadvantages with regard to earnings power. And anyway, the high cost of capital always gave the banks cause to complain.

Experience has shown that the pronounced and greatly simplified image of banks that prevailed on the stock market, one based to a considerable extent on an anticipation of the future, is very much at variance with actual banking practices, whether local, regional or national. The pluralistic structure in banking (public-sector savings banks and cooperative banks account for more than three-quarters of the banking sector) itself explains differences in practice.

To check the confusion this generated, private banks have endeavoured at all times to keep the image they portrayed of themselves, and in particular the portrayal of their strategic positions, to an absolute minimum in their stock market reports. Instead, they preferred to place emphasis on innovative improvements in advertising. In order to offer potential critics as few points of attack as possible the banks chose, moreover, to convey a completely vague universal bank idea that largely corresponded with the image of the sector as a whole and meant, more or less, finding new ways of expressing the status quo in the German banking industry.

Whether, however, this image can be preserved after Basle II is introduced in 2007 or whether it will have to undergo extensive changes is probably more of a rhetorical question. Compared to earlier times, the unconditionality and directness with which analysts and journalists, armed with legally prescribed ratios, will then demand details is likely to be a novel experience for Europeans. Top management may well be expected to provide, whether via roadshows or interviews, information at relatively short intervals that will not be confined solely to figures on recent business developments but will also have to include an exhaustive account of relevant strategic premises.

Besides the earnings per share, the optimal combination of business fields in the post-universal banking era is likely to become an issue for debate. Among bank shares, different combinations of business operations (each with its own individual evaluation) could soon come about. The results of these evaluations, sorted according to price performance, would then be discussed on a daily basis. In meetings with trade journalists, the explanations and justifications proffered by the main rivals would then be scrutinized and compared, and this, in turn, would undoubtedly have an impact on subsequent price performance. There may well be fewer and fewer advocates of universal banking in future, since they will probably be less and less able to deny accusations that unprofitable divisions are being subsidized. After all, accusations of this kind can only be refuted by facts.

Once the mist surrounding the preferences of the stock market has lifted and it is clear which decisions will be well-received and which will not, directors will probably have no alternative other than to recognize these principles. In other words, they will have to state unequivocally what combination of banking activities they intend to pursue in the longer term, and what divisions do not fit – and therefore will not feature – in the future concept.

Will international strategic alliances regain relevance as the competitive situation in banking re-forms?

As we have seen, two factors will have a key impact on competition in banking both at national and at international level: the system of the 'glass' bank after Basle II and indirect control via the stock markets. Any banking-arm-specific activities that lack promise will be regarded as 'dead weight' thrown overboard. The end of this structural selection process will be a relentless 'beauty contest' in search of the 'ideal figure' for a banking institution. As this process of 'clearing out' continues, notions of strategic recipes once justified as a safeguard against risk resulting from a possible structural change will be frowned upon as antiquated. To put it in general terms, the prevailing opinion is likely to be that the future belongs to the simple 'combination of active components'.

In the event that, as a result of unexpected economic developments, previously discarded lines of business again acquire an attractive earnings potential, the question will be whether these operations should again be cultivated and slowly allowed to grow, or whether the gap in the bank's product range might not be closed some other way. If a bank, for fear of making a wrong investment, is loath to decide to take over another company or merge with an attractive partner, the strategic alliance presents itself as a middle course, enabling the companies concerned to pool their know-how and set up joint places of operation manned by specially recruited staff.

Assuming the resultant mix of operative instruments is well-received by the market – probably also beyond the national borders – it may be advisable to switch to a full-scale merger at some point so that the shared success already achieved may be secured by paring organizational costs. The merged company could go on to take new strength from the successful alliance and present itself in a new form across Europe (which is to say that, driven by an external growth process, it could follow a development reminiscent of the early days of the universal banking era).

However, to make such an alliance as promising as possible from the outset it would be essential to develop lucid and detailed concrete objectives to allow the desired complementarity of both parties' business potentials to kick in as soon as possible. In other words, a cooperation of this kind would need to be tested step by step, analysed and underscored by an outwardly visible willingness to invest.

Those who flinch from such far-reaching consequences in the international business sector are indicating that they do not wish to overtax their base in the home market because they consider it potentially capable of further expansion. Certainly, strategic alliances entered into purely as a precautionary measure are not practical as they may be interpreted by the market as a sign that the potential partners do not necessarily need each other after all.

If, on the other hand, a strategic alliance seems a strategically indispensable means of pursuing top-priority business-policy objectives, the banks concerned should devote all their efforts to tailoring the alliance to its specific purpose at the first attempt, and to setting up joint units straight away on a trial basis. A dynamic upswing of this kind, which (as it were) outwardly announces itself, is the best way to create a constructive myth in the market. However, that myth will not come into full bloom until the public has been convinced of the significant advantages both parties can derive from putting the strategic alliance into operation.

The fact that Basle II will be adopted and implemented by all the industrial nations may be interpreted as an encouraging sign that throughout the world economic environment the tendency to invest in bank shares will pick up in the foreseeable future. The more reorganized, streamlined banks take a chance on strategic alliances with foreign partners in response to new developments at an international level, the more likely it is that they will participate in a new upturn of the banking sector as a whole.

Epilogue: Tombstones

The facination current events in the international community have for the average man or woman at first impact is out of all proportion to the contempt with which the same people cast these events from their minds only days or even hours later. The yearning enthusiasm initially bestowed upon things from beyond the home front, with which they are familiar to the point of satiation, which then gives way to indifference as information from abroad is quickly sorted out and erased from their memory. Yet those same people never tire of asserting how heavily their fate – as consumers and producers of goods – hinges on events outside their national borders.

The expert's backward view is indispensable also in economic life as a means of creating a balance, within the meaning of a harmonious co-existence, between local and global influences. Strongly simplifying clichés, and the simple blanking out of the same as competition-neutral factors, are of little help in this connection, as a relentless competitive battle is clearly raging on all sides between geographically and culturally restricted suppliers of internationally available product ranges, whereby the latter often have the initial advantage of a more effective public image.

Science is alone in a position, as umpire and chronicler, to provide clarity by determining and exposing, through ruthless comparison of causes and effects, typical characteristics of such undertakings. In the process, science also fulfils an economic need, namely of preventing the authors of trans-national business initiatives of outdated content from engaging in a cheerfully deceptive display of progressiveness for reasons of their own self-image, putting valuable economic resources at risk all the while. All too often, the whole show is a ploy to distract from crises on the home market, in the occurrence of which the same companies themselves played a part.

Since it is difficult to differentiate between actual and sham innovations without scientific proof, a worthwhile way of resolving this problem might be to set up a virtual graveyard of honour for abandoned cross-border strategic alliances, for the design and updating of which science ought to accept responsibility. The erection of virtual gravestones with the appropriate engravings would make it easier to document certain lines of development inasmuch as these inscriptions would state the ambitions that united the partners of the alliance as well as the results actually achieved. What is more, contributions rendered in the sector of trans-national alliances could be given recognition in the form of such virtual headstones, which in turn would attract a growing public interest. The sheer limitlessness of a virtual graveyard would be apt, moreover, in the absence of an endpoint to the development. After all, it will be easy for mystically driven market forces to revive tendencies of this kind, whatever the macroeconomic cycle. And if a standard of comparison were needed, the lifespan of an alliance could serve as a measure of soundness.

As far as BNP and Dresdner, the laureates, are concerned, it remains to be said that their main ambition lay in their belief that, by virtue of their position as second-biggest bank in their home markets, each with a global branch network at its disposal, they could prove to an eagerly awaiting world that there is no significant difference between the cross-border movement of goods and cross-border service-providing systems. For both could expand indefinitely – without any rigorous constraints – abroad. By burden of their proof the partners sought to herald a breakthrough to a new era, to mark a development that would lay open the road via a pan-European bank to a global, cosmopolitan bank.

Both banks persisted with their joint undertaking, bravely and honourably, for almost a decade; they had the chance to live out their creative drive within a superordinate framework, and also won recognition for their efforts. As an experiment, their alliance was important inasmuch as the banks struggled doggedly with the pitfalls of the task at hand to reach the above-mentioned insight. In this they were like the fairy-tale hero who must come through various adventures on his travels abroad only to find that his true place was at home all the time.

The fact that they did not comment in detail on this decision after the end of the alliance was officially announced does not in itself justify criticism, as they have not yet had an opportunity to do so. After all, they have all their energy focused on the tasks of the day, namely of defining new horizons to ensure the prosperity of their respective companies now and in the future.

Appendix 1:
Summary of the Cooperation Agreement between Banque Nationale de Paris and Dresdner Bank, 7 October 1996

Introduction

The Cooperation Agreement, summarized in this Appendix, grew out of the collaboration momentum that prevailed in 1991–2. The draft was presented to the European Commission on 27 January 1993 so as to form the basis of its deliberations on the proposed strategic alliance.

The Agreement was officially signed on 7 October 1996. The context within which the Agreement had been drafted had changed, but nevertheless the nature of the Agreement (consisting of broad phrases not implying any specific programme of activities) allowed its continued validity. The official signing signalled the start of the alliance and the initiatives executed were those considered appropriate to the 1996 context.

Summary

The Cooperation Agreement between Banque Nationale de Paris and Dresdner Bank Aktiengellschaft consisted of a preamble, 28 Sections and a number of associated, clarifying, Annexes.

Preamble

The cooperation is based on the long-standing relations between the two banks and will contribute to the development of ties between France and Germany, the European Union and the global banking environment. The cooperation will reduce costs, allow exchange of use of networks and thereby enable the provision of services at attractive and competitive prices to their customers, though returns may be differential.

A – General

Section 1 – Universal cooperation.
Cooperation will be universal as equal partners, though specific areas may be excluded and each partner will retain their own corporate identity.

Section 2 – Exclusivity
The cooperation is exclusive to the founding partners and any conflict of interest is to be jointly resolved.

Section 3 – Information and confidentially
Information exchange is being encouraged at all levels and be subject to confidentiality and due diligence.

Section 4 – Cross-participation
In addition to the nomination of a 'Director of BNP to Dresdner Bank's Supervisory Board and a Director of Dresdner Bank to BNP's Board of Directors' a maximum share cross-holding of 10 per cent will be established at the appropriate time.

B – Objectives of the cooperation

Section 5 – General business objectives
To reduce costs, manage risks and provide competitively priced products while allowing greater use of each other's branch networks. To focus on return on equity rather than business volume and balance retention of profits by joint ventures and distribution of profits to the parent companies.

Section 6 – Objectives regarding activities in France and Germany
Each partner is to allow the other to use their branch networks, to assist in developing services, and precluded from competing, or collaborating with those competing, with the partner in their home country.

Section 7 – Objectives regarding activities in countries other than France and Germany (hereinafter called 'third countries').
The partners will set up joint units in third countries, as jointly agreed.

Section 8 – The holding
All joint ventures will be constituted as separate companies with their own funds, developing their own identity and will be registered as banks.

Section 9 – Representative offices
A coordinated approach and, where possible, sharing of offices should be the norm in opening representative offices.

Section 10 – Disposal of third country investments
No disposal, in whole or in part, to a third party should take place without the consent of the other partner. The partner has first refusal to purchase the shares of the other partner in a disposal situation.

C – Specific areas of cooperation

Section 11 – Objectives regarding international financings
Partners act in the market as one entity.

Section 12 – Merchant banking, securities, asset management and investment banking
Partners develop synergies to obtain better performance.

D – Support areas

Section 13 – Organizational matters
Partners establish common premises, election data processing and support strategies.

Section 14 – Personnel
Staff exchanges between partners to engender a cooperative stance in corporate culture.

Section 15 – Public relations, advertising and internal communication
Partners to promote a national and international common cooperative image.

Section 16 – Internal auditing
Partners to exchange information to harmonize audit methods in relation to joint ventures.

Section 17 – Accounting, reporting and controlling
Partners to develop common rules for reporting and for internal control systems.

E – The regulatory bodies of the cooperation

Section 18 – The regular meetings
Partners to hold bi-annual meetings of the Boards of BNP and Dresdner together to discuss cooperative strategy and agree amendments to the Cooperation Agreement. Decisions to be unanimous.

Section 19 – The commission
A commission of an equal number of representatives from each partner to be set up.

Section 20 – The cooperation secretariat
A secretariat with equal representation to be set up.

F – Miscellaneous

Section 21 – Amendment
Regular reviews of the agreement to be conducted that partners may amend at any time.

Section 22 – Annexes
Annexes A to F are integral to the Agreement.

Section 23 – Disputes and termination
Termination clauses going through levels – secretariat, commission, partners meeting, International Chamber of Commerce, arbitration under Swiss law, one-year notice of termination by either partner.

Section 24 – Language
Agreement made in French, German and English. Latter predominant in case of disputes.

Section 25 – Partial invalidity or unenforceability
If any part of the Agreement becomes invalidated, new conditions may be substituted, and the rest of the Agreement remains unaffected.

Section 26 – Scope of agreement
Agreement is binding on partners, successors and assignees.

Section 27 – Applicable law
Agreement under the laws of Switzerland.

Section 28 – Coming into force
7 October 1996.

Signatures

Banque Nationale de Paris   *Dresdner Bank AG*
Michel Pébereau   Jürgen Sarrazin
Jacques Henri Wahl   Piet-Jochen Etzel

Annexes

These provide more detail to the Sections of the Agreement.

Appendix 2:
Official Journal of the European Communities, Information and Notices, C312, 23 November 1995*

Notice pursuant to Article 19 (3) of Council Regulation No 17 concerning Case No IV/34.607, Banque Nationale de Paris–Dresdner Bank (95/C 312/08) (Text with EEA relevance)

The Facts

1. The notified cooperation agreement

1. *The notification*
The cooperation agreement was formally notified to the Commission of the European Communities on 27 January 1993 in accordance with Articles 2 and 4 of Council Regulation No 17 (OJ No 13. 21. 2. 1962, p. 204/62). It provides for full and, in principle, exclusive cooperation worldwide between Banque Nationale de Paris (BNP) and Dresdner Bank (DB) in the banking sector. It is of indefinite duration and was approved at the annual general meetings of the two banks.

2. *The aims of the cooperation*
– The two banks wish to meet the growing challenge in the banking sector that is posed by new competitors such as foreign banks, insurance companies, companies with their own in-house banks, and also the credit card companies that are offering an ever-expanding range of financial services. To that end, the two banks plan to achieve synergies in order to reduce costs, chiefly through very close cooperation in logistics and certain international activities.

– The two banks wish to meet the challenges of the single market and the globalization of markets where customers are increasingly requiring international financial services. They therefore plan to strengthen their presence in all countries other than France and Germany (third countries) in order both to compete more strongly with foreign banks and to offer their customers in France and Germany a much wider range of international financial services.

---

*Reproduced from *Official Journal of the European Communities*, C312, 23 November 1995, with permission.

3. *Concept underlying the cooperation*
BNP and DB both wish to remain:
– leading universal banks in their home markets,
– in the single European market, leading universal banks with branches or subsidiaries in at least the major European countries,
– present in all the major financial centers, offering appropriate services.
4. *The four areas of cooperation*
(a) Cooperation in organizational matters and through the exchange of information
In order to achieve synergies, reduce costs and risks and improve customer services, the cooperation agreement provides for some harmonization of the two banks' organization, in particular through the exchange of information and the joint development of data-processing instruments, office automation and economic data. Agreement was also reached on setting up the appropriate agreements and technical means for reducing transfer costs and times for cross-frontier payments. The partners will also exchange staff and consult each other before any public announcements, including advertising and publicity about their cooperation.

There will also be an exchange of information on economic and general subjects and on new business opportunities, new products or specialized financing techniques.
(b) Specific areas of cooperation
In the field of international financing, the partners, their structures in 'third countries' and the holding company in which they will place their 'third country' business at the appropriate time (see paragraph (c)) will be arranged so as to be perceived by the market as being a single entity. They will invite each other to participate in all types of financing (direct loans, leasing, financial instruments or other arrangements) in which banks other than domestic banks are involved. A partner requested to participate in this way may refuse to participate in the proposed financing only on reasonable grounds, which must be explained to the other party. If other financial institutions invite one of the partners to form a syndicate, that party must make every effort to ensure that the other is also invited.

As regards merchant banking, capital markets and the placing of securities in 'third countries', the partners will cooperate in the search for synergies and savings in the development of new products and in order to maximize investments.

As regards securities and their placing, derivatives, asset management and investment banking, the two banks will cooperate without geographical limits. The form of cooperation depends on the actual product: it may involve the development of new products or strategies, concerted marketing or the exchange of information.
(c) Cooperation in activities outside France and Germany (third countries)
This area of cooperation is aimed at expanding the two banks' scope for providing their customers with international financial services by improving and regrouping their structures in those countries.

To that end, they agree to identify synergies and, in time, to combine their existing banking activities in 'third countries', with the exception of the United States of America. This may in particular be achieved by merging operations within one or more joint subsidiaries, by acquiring a 50 holding in a partner's subsidiary or eventually by establishing a joint holding company which would initially be a financial holding company and could eventually become a fully operational bank.

The partners will notify any new activities and discuss them with each other on the basis of a feasibility study, in order to reach harmonized conclusions. The other party will be invited to participate in such activities. The offer may be rejected by the partner only for very substantial reasons.

If a partner wishes to dispose of its share of a joint activity, it requires the express agreement of the other party. A holding that is to be sold must first be offered to the partner. If a partner wishes to sell an entity which it wholly owns, it must inform the other partner and allow it to express an opinion.

As regards cooperation between the partners, the holding company and structures in 'third countries', the agreement provides that if a partner does not have the means of supplying a customer with the appropriate service for an international transaction, it must refer the customer to its partner. The partners are also required to grant credit to each other's customers in countries where one or the other does not engage in such activities, subject to terms and possibly guarantees to be agreed jointly by all the parties concerned. Interbanking activities (exchange transactions, securities, options, futures, swaps, etc.) by bodies involved in the cooperation must also be given priority by each partner, provided that the transaction is offered at competitive rates.

The offices representing the two partners in 'third countries' will be physically merged whilst retaining autonomy and their own identity, except in cases where it seems preferable to have a single joint office.

If one of the partners (the informing party) wishes to conclude a cooperation agreement with a third party, whether or not limited sectorally or geographically, it must inform the other partner (the informed party) of its intention. If the latter does not agree, it must give its reasons. If the informing party, after duly considering the reasons given by the informed party for its refusal, intends to pursue its plan and if the proposed agreement does not affect any vital interests of the informed party but could on the contrary be vital to the informing party, the latter is free to act as it wishes.

(d) Cooperation on the French and German markets

This area of cooperation is aimed at increasing the range of services available through the two networks and thus improving the competitiveness of the two banks.

To that end each partner undertakes to make available to the other all its services at the best price and in turn to offer its own customers the widest possible range of the services provided by its partner. As a result of their joint activities in 'third countries', the two banks will be able to offer their customers at home a range of new services from those countries.

As regards the activities of the two banks on their home markets, the agreement provides that the partners are free to act as they wish, unless one of them wishes to conclude a cooperation with a home country competitor: before concluding such an agreement, it must inform its partner.

If a partner is unable to provide its home customers with an international service, it must call on the other partner, or one of the structures in a 'third country', or the holding company, once the latter has become a fully operational bank.

With regard to the question of the partners' activities on each other's home markets, the cooperation agreement does not restrict access to such markets through existing subsidiaries or prohibit the creation of new subsidiaries or branches or the acquisition by one partner of a competitor on the other's domestic market. On the other hand, it does limit the extent to which one partner may operate on the other's domestic market by cooperating with a competitor of the latter; agreements with a partner's domestic competitor may only be concluded with the latter's express consent. More specifically, if one partner is considering concluding a cooperation agreement, even one that is limited geographically or sectorally, with a third party, it must inform the other partner of its intention. If the latter fails to agree it must state its reasons to the former.

Whereas the agreement initially notified to the Commission gave the informed party the absolute right to withhold approval (Annex A.1, paragraph 3, last sentence), the two banks agreed, in response to a request by the Commission, to limit this right of absolute and irreversible refusal to cases where a cooperation agreement with a third party involves the utilization of know-how or business secrets which the informant has received from the informed party or which results from the cooperation. 'Know-how' in this context is the know-how as defined in Article 1 of Commission Regulation (EEC) No 556/89 of 30 November 1988 on the application of Article 85 (3) of the Treaty to certain categories of know-how licensing agreements (OJ No L 61, 4. 3. 1989. p. 1.). This limit on the right to refuse approval to cooperation between one of the banks with a domestic competitor of the other bank will be clarified in an annex to the cooperation agreement.

The consent of the partner is not required in the day-to-day trading activities, although each must give the other preferential treatment in this area. Nor is a partner's consent required where it has not taken part in such an agreement, having exercised its right of refusal.

5. *The structures set up by the agreement*

The BNP and DB Management Boards will meet twice a year to decide on joint strategy and to take unanimous decisions on any proposals relating to the notified cooperation agreement submitted to them by a committee.

That committee, which will meet three times a year and be chaired alternately by the two banks, will define priorities and the measures to be taken by the two partners. It must, in particular, examine the recommendations of a secretariat and submit proposed amendments to the agreement at bi-annual meetings of the BNP and DB Boards.

That cooperation secretariat will be composed of representatives of the two banks. It must assist the partners in the practical implementation of the cooperation, but must also make recommendations relating to necessary improvements to the agreement, which it must submit to the Committee.

6. *Cross-boldings*

The partners plan to strengthen their cooperation at the appropriate time by establishing cross-shareholdings of 10 per cent of the issued shares.

2. Current relations between BNP and DB

7. BNP and DB agreed in the past to appoint a Director of BNP to DB's Supervisory Board and a Director of DB to BNP's Board of Directors.

They also created a joint venture to gain access to the market of former Czechoslovakia. BNP and DB each hold 37 per cent of BNP–KH–Dresdner Bank RT in Hungary, 26 per cent of which is held by Országos Kereskedelmi és Hitelbank RL

The two transactions were authorized by the Commission (Cases (IV/MTF/021 and IV/MTF/124).

BNP and DB also have joint holdings in the following:

– United Overseas Bank, Geneva, Lugano, Luxembourg, Monaco, Bahamas, Montevideo: BNP and DB each hold 50 per cent,

– BNP–AK–Dresdner Bank AS Istanbul, Iszmir: BNP 30 per cent, DB 30 per cent and AK-Bank Group 40 per cent,

– Société Financiére pour les Pays d'Outre-mer, with activities in Africa: BNP 48,4 per cent; DB 25,8 per cent and BBL 25,8 per cent,

– BNP–Dresdner Bank (Polska) SA, Warsaw: BNP 50 per cent and DB 50 per cent,

– BNP–Dresdner Bank (Russia), St Petersburg (together with a branch in Moscow); BNP 33 per cent, Dresdner Bank 33 per cent Europabank (wholly owned by DB) 17 per cent and SFA (Société Financière Auxiliére, Paris, wholly owned by BNP) 17 per cent,

– BNP–Dresdner Bank (Bulgaria) AD, Sofia: BNP and DB each hold 40 per cent and EBR 20 per cent

3. The enterprises parties to the notified agreement and their position on the financial markets

8. *Banque Nationale de Paris*

BNP SA is a full-service bank operating directly or indirectly through subsidiaries, chiefly in France, Europe, French-speaking countries and worldwide. In Germany, it owns a branch in Frankfurt with two agencies attached. It also has a subsidiary there, specializing in mergers and acquisitions.

Its total consolidated balance sheet in 1994 (1993) was ECU222 (224) billion. Of its 54,469 (56,141) employees, 13,169 (13,851) work abroad. BNP has a total of 2,511 (2,575) offices worldwide, of which 497 (567) are outside France.

The BNP group wholly owns Natio-Vie, a life insurance company. Together with UAP it created a joint venture, Natio-Assurance, to market UAP's non-life insurance.

The capital is held as follows:

14,32 per cent	UAP
15,48 per cent	core capital shareholders
2,31 per cent	French State
67,89 per cent	public.

On the basis of its total consolidated balance sheet for 1993, BNP ranks fourth in France, seventh in Europe and nineteenth worldwide.

9. *Dresdner Bank*

Dresdner Bank AG is a full-service bank which operates directly or indirectly through subsidiaries, chiefly in Germany but also in other European and non-European countries. Two of its subsidiaries are in France, one being the Banque Veuve Morin-Pons SA with branches in Paris, Lyon and Strasbourg. The other is the Banque Internationale de Placement, Paris.

Its total consolidated balance sheet in 1994 (1993) was ECU210 (197) billion. Of its 44,884 employees (1994), some 3,000 work abroad. Of a total of 1,583 branches, 58 are outside Germany.

Dresdner Bank operates in some Länder in Germany as a distributor of insurance contracts for Allianz and, in others, for Hamburg-Mannheimer.

The capital is held as follows:

21,97 per cent	Allianz AG Holding
10,60 per cent	FGF Frankfurter Gesellschaft für Finanzwerte mbH
10,58 per cent	Vermo Vermögensverwaltungsgesellschaft mbH
1,90 per cent	employees and pensioners
54,95 per cent	general public and institutional investors.

On the basis of the 1993 balance sheet, DB ranks second in Germany, 12th in Europe and twenty-sixth worldwide.

4. The position of both banks in the countries making up the EEA in 1994

10. The notified cooperation has an impact on all the activities of both banks. It will, in practice, affect virtually all the financial services markets on which the two banks operate, with the exception of the insurance services market.

As a general rule, each type of banking service is offered both to commercial custom-ers (including banks) and to individuals and small firms. Customers in the first cat-egory are able, because of their experience of financial markets and the staff and resources they can use, to gain access to the financial markets at European, or even world level, but private customers do not on the whole have access to banking net-works outside their country of residence.

The following table shows the position of both banks in various countries of the EEA, all activities being aggregated. The percentages show the position of BNP and Dresdner Bank in these countries if we make a country-by-country comparison of the market share held by each of the two banks with the total market share held by all banks:

Country	BNP	Dresdner Bank
France	approximately 7 per cent	under 1 per cent
Germany	under 1 per cent	approximately 5 per cent
Luxembourg	under 3 per cent	approximately 5 per cent

Note: the exact figures are business secrets.

In other EEA countries, the position of each bank, apart from BNP in Ireland, is negli-gible, being under 1,4 per cent in two cases (DB in Ireland and BNP in Greece), and not above 1 per cent in the other cases.

In the five principal areas of banking (loans to banks, loans to customers, securities, bank deposits and customer deposits), the respective positions of BNP and DB do not vary by more than two percentage points from the figures indicated above.

The market shares for 1994 are as follows:

German market

According to the details provided for 46 different banking services, DB's shares of the markets for services to individuals and small firms in a few cases exceed the figure stated above by some two percentage points and, in just one case, by some five per-centage points, whilst in most cases the figure is below the percentage indicated above. On the other hand, its share of the commercial customer's markets in most cases considerably exceeds the above figure of some 5 per cent. In the case of two banking services offered to commercial customers, DB's share even reaches some 20 per cent.

The position of BNP with regard to the various services it offers on the German market is negligible.

French market

The details supplied for 26 markets indicate that BNP's share of the markets for ser-vices supplied to individuals and small firms differs only slightly from the figure given above. In only one market does it achieve about 10 per cent. Its shares of the market for the services offered to commercial customers are slightly higher than those stated above, except in one case where its market share amounts to some 20 per cent.

The share of all the markets held by DB in France is negligible.

Luxembourg market

According to the figures provided for five types of services, in one case DB holds some 11 per cent of the relevant market, in two cases below 5 per cent and in two cases a very light share.

The figures provided for BNP for the same five services are in one case under 3 per cent, in three cases under 1.5 per cent and in one case under 8 per cent, whereas the position of DB in this area is roughly 11 per cent.

5. Conclusion

In view of the foregoing and in particular the undertaking of the two banks to limit the scope of the clause allowing one partner to prevent the other from concluding any cooperation agreement with a domestic competitor of the former, the Commission intends to adopt a favourable position with regard to the notified agreement.

Before doing so, it invites interested parties to send their comments within one month of the date of publication of this notice in the *Official Journal of the European Communities*, quoting reference TV/34,607, to the following address:

Commission of the European Communities,
Directorate-General for Competition (DG IV),
Directorate IV/D — Services,
Rue de la Loi/Wetstraat 200,
B-1049 Brussels.

Appendix 3:
Stages of the Partnership between BNP and Dresdner Bank

September 1988	BNF–AK-Dresdner Bank AS, Istanbul
June 1989	Exchange of mandates: Mr Wahl as a member of the Supervisory board of Dresdner Bank and Mr Sarrazin as a member of the Board of directors of BNP
June 1991	BNP–KH-Dresdner Bank RT, Budapest
May 1992	BNP–Dresdner (CSFR) AS Prague
May 1993	Approval of the suggested agreement by the General shareholders' meeting of the Dresdner Bank
May 1993	Approval of the suggested agreement by the shareholders of the Banque Nationale de Paris
November 1993	BNP–Dresdner Bank (Rossija), St Petersburg
January 1995	BNP–Dresdner Bank (Polska) SA, Varchow
July 1995	BNP–Dresdner Bank (Bulgaria), Sofia
November 1995	Clearance of the cooperation agreement by the European Commission
May 1996	Dresdner–Banque Nationale de Paris, Santiago de Chile
October 1996	Signing of the cooperation agreement in Paris
September 1997	BNP–Dresdner Bank (Croatia) DD, Zagreb
October 1998	BNP–Dresdner Bank (Romania) SA, Bucharest
January 1999	BNP–Dresdner European Bank AG, Vienna
June 2001	Agreement on dissolving the joint ventures
October 2002	Cooperation agreement between BNP and Dresdner Bank officially terminated

Index